YOUNG WRITERS

Spellbound

HEREFORD & WORCESTER

Edited by Simon Harwin

First published in Great Britain in 1998 by
POETRY NOW YOUNG WRITERS
1-2 Wainman Road, Woodston,
Peterborough, PE2 7BU
Telephone (01733) 230748

HB ISBN 0 754 300 269
SB ISBN 0 754 300 277

FOREWORD

In this, our 5th competition year, we are proud to present *Spellbound Hereford & Worcester*. This anthology represents the very best endeavours of the children from this region.

The standard of entries was high, which made the task of editing a difficult one, but nonetheless enjoyable. The variety of subject matter, creativity and imagination never ceases to amaze and is indeed an inspiration to us all.

This year's competition attracted the highest entry ever - over 46,000 from all over the UK, and for the first time included entries from English speaking children living abroad.

Congratulations to all the writers published in *Spellbound Hereford & Worcester*. We hope you enjoy reading the poems and that your success will inspire you to continue writing in the future.

CONTENTS

Rebeka Ellam   68

Burlish Middle School
                Ellie Southall   69
                Louise Broadley   69
                Emma Rainsford   70
                Sarah Smith   70
                Gemma Shaw   71
                Luke Martin   72
                Lauren Bucceri   72
                Mark Harrodine   73
                Rachel Pitman   73
                Bradlie Bucceri   74
                Sarah Taylor   74
                Scott Bentley   75
                Philip Baldwin   75
                Robert Phillips   76
                David Ireland   76
                Andrew Butler   77
                Sadie Tandy   77
                Charlotte Harris   78
                Craig Johnstone   78
                Martha Clingan   79
                Natasha Beddard   79
                Cheryl Adams   80
                Claire Williams   80
                Emily Hobson   81
                Laura Southall   81
                Melissa Pearson   82
                Natasha Noyes   82
                Joanne Portman   83
                Julie Longmore   83
                Melissa Kennedy   84
                Kerri Duce   84
                Laura K Hobbs   85
                Sam Hibbert   85
                Phillipa Smith   86

Max Westwood	86
Deborah Clarke	87
Josh Vale	88
Jamie Bevans	88
Victoria Rodwell	89
Natalie Bishop	89
Carla Valler-Jones	90
Rob Williams	90
Nikki Greenwood	91
Stacey Green	92
Catherine Homer	92
Claire Charlwood	93
Helen Poulton	93
Lucie Nelson	94
Emma Mayo	94

Christopher Whitehead High School

| Alison Higgins | 95 |
| Jodie Marie Rice | 96 |

Comberton Middle School

Thomas Siviter	96
Peter Mason	97
Clare Millard	98
Adam Chester	98
Lowri Garrant	99
Sarah McKeown	100
John Pochribniak	100
Paul Brookes	101
Paul Lovell	102
Susan Baker	102
Nicholas J Crumpton	103
Thomas Lai	104
Gemma Smith	105
Louise Howes	105
Hayley Slater	106
Emily Markham	106

David Koker	107
Laura Thomas	108
Katie Andrews	108
David Lane	109
Richard Anderson	110
Catriona Malcolm	110
Gemma Davies	111
Tim Willetts	112
Adele Cro	112
Andrew Ireland	113
Matthew Vaughan	114
Gemma Cannock	114
Charlotte Waldron	115
Jonathan Buckerfield	116
David Cadwallader	117
Sam Beasley	118
Thomas Brown	118
Sarah Handley	119
Naomi Jarman	120
Mark Jones	121
Louise Allchurch	122
Chris MacDonald	123
Gemma Parker	124

Fairfield High School

James Brookes	124
Amy Wheeler	125
Joanne Edwards	125
Tavline McDonough	126
Rachel Price-Greenow	126
Christopher Jenkins	127
Tom Ward	128
Gemma A Weeks	128
Natalie Mark	129
Rebecca Jones	129
Llewelyn Watkins	130
Paul Archer	130

St John's CE Middle School

Mark Caseley	175
Timothy Maughan	176
Anna Ostrowski	176
Eleanor Morgan	177
Catherine Furey	178
Christine Weston	178
Holly Maund	179
Ashley Rollings	179
Lisa Mills	180
Jennifer Macdonald	180
Kayleigh Pearson	181
Jolene Nutting	182
Sam Flory	183
Annabel Webb	184
Aimeé Rollings	184
Samir Hissaund	185
Natalie Duce	186
Kris Brown	186
Laura Stickley	187
Stacey Baker	188
Christy Archer	189
Michelle Heeley	190
Daniel Bate	190
Louise Fuller	191
Bonnie Heath	192
Catherine Luke	192
James Phillips	193
Alison Common	194
Ben Taylor	194
Katie Chandler	195
Laura Skirving	195
Alex Jordan	196
James Page	196
Rebekah Lane	197
Freja Dommett	198
Rachel Smith	199

THE POEMS

LITTLE FLOWER

Flowers are pretty
Yellow and blue
Rounded and smooth
Fine and delicate.
Bright!
Facing to the sun,
collecting its good energy.
Sunbathing!
Nimble little face glittering,
Twisting to the sun.
Colourful and attractive
Tiny and small
Sweetly scented
Like perfume
Thirst quenching
Dances!
They love the sun.

Clare Westoby (12)
Bishop of Hereford's Bluecoat School

SLAVERY

S laves silently walking with bare feet on the parched ground
L oneliness in the air as their daily routine is carried out
A fter their dinner of corn meal mush they go back to their
     draughty, dirty cabins
V ery slowly the slaves get to sleep and rest their aching bodies
E verybody is woken before five in the morning to start their
     day's work
R eally hot days spent reaching up high picking the white bolls
Y oung as two and old as eighty all dreading the awful whip.

Sophie Thompson (12)
Bishop of Hereford's Bluecoat School

SPACE

Darkness,
Stretching into eternity,
Masses of rock hurtling throughout,
Beacons of light,
Piercing the blackness,
Waves of colour,
Washing into the inky nothingness,
Unspoiled beauty,
Mystical and indestructible,
Forever growing,
Impossible,
But it's out there,
And we call it space.

John Driessen (13)
Bishop of Hereford's Bluecoat School

LANDMINES

Landmines, no thanks, not on my land,
I think they ought to be banned.

Who needs them anyway?
In the end somebody has to pay.

Causing death and terrible grief,
Usually there is no relief.

Will it be an arm or leg?
The rest of your life walking on a peg.

Ban them and stop this maiming,
Let us not feel this awful shaming.

James Young (12)
Bishop of Hereford's Bluecoat School

FOXES

Red foxes brown,
With big bushy tails
Night-hunters
Rarely seen in daylight.
At the top of the food chain
But hound hunted.
Ripped apart by hungry hounds.
Bloodied coat and flesh,
And powerful legs, useless.

Foxes kill!
It's nature.
Chickens they hunt.
they have to eat
Like you and me.

In the spring and summer
The cubs are born,
Playing happily together
Contented, growing up,
Safe in the country.
Soon they leave their parents
Like you and me.

They are night animals,
Secret animals,
Killed some day.

Jenny Hall (12)
Bishop of Hereford's Bluecoat School

BLACK DIRT

Take a look at me,
You'd see a cripple,
Take a look at me,
You'd look away.
I used to laugh and dance and sing,
But now I've lost my everything.
My life, my world, forever scarred,
Not just my torn black skin,
But my large, black soul has been ripped away from me,
Bit by bit.

Past that tall mud wall,
Is a world that treats you fair,
But no one that I know would dare,
To cross that fateful line.
For their life,
Is ruled by one small fear,
That whip that could skin a back
In just one angry, vicious lash,
That fear,
The 'Cat o'nine tails'.

Simon Davies (12)
Bishop of Hereford's Bluecoat School

THE SWAN

The swan is beautiful in every way,
Her gorgeous pure white wings glistening in the sun.
Gliding over the icy, blue water,
Gracefully as she goes.

She suddenly dives down into the water,
Bringing up a silver salmon,
All the colours of the rainbows.

Lizzy King (12)
Bishop of Hereford's Bluecoat School

THE RED-HAIRED BOY

The boy with the red hair,
Sitting in the corner.
No one likes him,
For he is so horrible.

But is he really,
Is he really horrible?
Or is he just lonely,
And wanting a friend?

He can't even kick a ball,
And he's useless at sport.
He works as hard as he can,
Even though he's in set four.

He spends all his time
In the library,
Reading a book in the corner,
Or he's playing on the computers.

Maybe one day he'll find a friend,
But for now, he's just,
The red-haired boy
Sitting in the corner.

Nicola Withford-Eaton (12)
Bishop of Hereford's Bluecoat School

LIFE AFTER HIS DEATH

Red eyes,
streaming with painful tears.
Broken hearts
that will not mend.
Numbness
that causes emotional silence.
Respect,
that was not there,
when he was alive.

Questions
that were never asked.
Love,
that was never expressed.
Hate,
that was never hidden.
Guilt,
that shall remain inside,
forever.

Hayley Hinksman (13)
Bishop of Hereford's Bluecoat School

NEW GROWTH

In small villages people are busy
With their everyday tasks.
War suddenly breaks out
Between them and villagers in another country.
Both sides soon find themselves without food,
So leave their homes.
The villages are deserted.
Silence.

A few years pass
Before signs of life show.
Flowers and crops grow,
A few people moving.
A decade passes
For everything to be how it was,
So once more people are busy
With their everyday tasks.

Rhian Hill (13)
Bishop of Hereford's Bluecoat School

HAIR

Why do we have hair?
Bald people seem OK.
They don't have all the hair hassles
Like nits, dandruff, bushy sticky frizzy
hair.

The things people do to their hair -
Old ladies dying their hair blue;
Shaved heads with gelled spikes;
Hair sprayed stiff like rocks - Yuk!

Without my hair I'd feel incomplete
I like to make it shiny and thick
If only it would be long and straight
Glossy and flowing and bouncy - like
the people on TV.

I'd like to try every style to
Change myself into different people
But whatever I do seems not me -
I keep on changing it to see what kind
of person I am.

Katy Sumner (13)
Bishop of Hereford's Bluecoat School

MY CAT TOBY

With no worries and no cares
He sprawls lazily on the carpet
Fur glinting as it catches the sunlight,
Claws spread, eyes closed.

Purring like a lawnmower
He pads over to me
Butting his small furry head
Against my leg lovingly.

He rolls over on his side
As I stroke his glossy coat.
My greatest possession,
My cat Toby.

Natalie King (13)
Bishop of Hereford's Bluecoat School

GOD

You're a thunderstorm of power,
A wave of control,
You're a sunshine of happiness,
The tree that never dies.
You're a war full of strength,
But you never get hurt.
You've a world full of people,
rolled into one.
So where are you when people die?
Why do you take them?
Just tell me that.

Sarah Caton (13)
Bishop of Hereford's Bluecoat School

FREEDOM

Wouldn't it be great
to be able
to take a day out and
just glide down an open freeway?
Perhaps route 66;
Palm trees either side,
Classy, elegant 'poodle walkers',
handsome, fit beach boys relaxing
in a game of volley ball,
all paused in their action.

Nothing in front,
Nothing behind.

Think of how many places you could
be in one time.
Sunbathing in the Caribbean,
Swimming in a pool surrounded
by deep blue dolphins.
Soaring like a bird on a thermal,
Skiing off piste down the famous Alps
of Switzerland,
Standing alone at the top of the Cairngorm
200 miles of Scotland in sight,
Meeting the man of your dreams
And spending a romantic night under the stars
or . . . .

Helena Sime (13)
Bishop of Hereford's Bluecoat School

ALL AROUND US

There are a million things going on.
I'm too ignorant,
Sightless and
Blind to see them.

I'm too oblivious,
Unhearing,
Deaf to hear them.

I'm too inarticulate,
Speechless and
Dumb to speak to them.

I'm too puny,
Weak,
Feeble to feel them.

There are a billion things going on,
Multitudes
Going on, this instant.

Right here
Right now
Right here
All around us.

Alex Carini (13)
Bishop of Hereford's Bluecoat School

FIRE!

It's like the devil all hot and red,
It spreads through the house. Are my family still in bed?
I go to the landing,
Where my family are standing.
Into my parents' room we all run
And climb through the window, one by one.

My dad runs round to my neighbour's house,
And phones the Fire Brigade,
Our house is going up in flames,
I'm scared, I'm scared but who is to blame?

Andrea Gummer *(12)*
Bishop of Hereford's Bluecoat School

SWEETS

Sweets are very delicious
Some are big and very tasty
And some are round

Sweets are in different shapes
Some are long and some are thin
Fat and some sweets
Are square shaped.

Some sweets come in different wrappers
Like sparkling inviting covers.
Pink
Blue
Or even sparkling yellow.

Some sweets are very tasty
Some taste of strawberry and
Others lime and blackberry
And other sweets are plain.

People would give anything
For just one sweet
Other sweets are sour
And other ones are sweet.

Steve Webb *(12)*
Bishop of Hereford's Bluecoat School

THE SPIDER

Scuttling making no sound
Silently breathing
Dark legs moving across the floor
Giant steps
Fear pours out like a waterfall
Hairs on the back of the neck
Standing tall like soldiers
Butterflies swarm around in the stomach
Suddenly black liquid darkens the room
Silence
A once living creature is no more
Silence is endless
Yet
The cold fear has vanished
Now there is nothing to fear
Or is there?

Kathryn Mellors (13)
Bishop of Hereford's Bluecoat School

THE WAVE

The strong waves which crash on the waiting rocks,
Breaking just a short distance from my feet.
The waves spraying the clear warm water over my foot.
The rushing water stops for a split second waiting . . .
Then it's off again,
Carrying the mixed salt and sand,
On its way.
Pulling any obstacles along
With the now gentle wave.

Vicky Woodfield (12)
Bishop of Hereford's Bluecoat School

THE SEA

You see,
a new universe,
engulfed by water,
slowly, slowly,
you float with its rhythm.

You hear,
the cries of a majestic whale,
a heartbroken whale,
slowly, slowly,
swimming out to sea.

You see,
hidden under the rocks,
a leaking barrel,
slowly, slowly,
poisoning this watery paradise.

Sophie Day (13)
Bishop Of Hereford's Bluecoat School

BULLY

He comes every Thursday after school,
And beats me to the ground,
The scars on his face and every little sound,
His uttered words makes me shiver all around,
I can't tell my parents,
I never will do,
Because he will get me,
And flush my head down the loo,
I hate him but I daren't make a sound,
One day I will and I will beat *him* to the ground.

Alice Pollock (13)
Bishop of Hereford's Bluecoat School

A REAL TEAM

The two cobs stand together,
Identical,
Restless,
Waiting for their driver.

They both feel a jolt.
They wait and listen;
Twenty-three is their number.
The steward starts calling.

The horses feel the tension,
Building, flowing through the reins,
Their hearts start throbbing,
23 . . . go

They head towards the trees,
Picking up speed;
Racing through the wood,
Sensitive of every move their driver makes.

They rely on him to guide them;
They obey his every command.
The crowd comes into sight;
They know what they have to do.

The pair give it everything they've got,
They feel their bodies tighten -
As they pass the finish line;
Then suddenly the strain has gone and it's all over.

Anna Baker (13)
Bishop of Hereford's Bluecoat School

THE SHEAF HORSES

The sun is setting,
Evening is drawing nigh,
The sunset's spectrum of colours
Make themselves known,
The rays of light strike the galloping horses,
As they seemingly run through the wheat field,
Galloping, chasing, leaping,
Knocking down the sheaves of wheat as they go.

Tiredness overwhelms them,
The wind dies down,
The horses come to a halt,
Everything becomes still again,
Until *next* time . . .

Heather Samuel (13)
Bishop of Hereford's Bluecoat School

IT'S A CAT'S LIFE

It's a cat's life,
They miaow for food,
and when that's done,
They sprawl and lounge out in the sun.
They rouse themselves and go and
hunt for
Mice or voles or even birds.
When they return a meal awaits,
They fill themselves and then recline,
It's a cat's life.

Jenny Preedy (13)
Bishop of Hereford's Bluecoat School

HAVING HAEMOPHILIA

I had a day off school today,
because I've got a bleed.
'Come here Sye,' Mum said to me,
'An injection is what you need!'
She mixed up all my treatment,
slid the needle into my arm;
I've gotta have these bloomin' things,
to stop me from coming to harm.
I suppose it isn't that bad really,
I can still play any game;
like playing soccer, running round,
I'm not completely lame!
I get loads of support from people I know,
from my friends and close family too.
So it seems there's nothing wrong with me,
there's nothing I can't do!

Simon Freeman (13)
Bishop of Hereford's Bluecoat School

THE NIGHT

I gaze out of the window,
Into the night skies,
Speckled with silvery stars.
All of a sudden
A bat swoops by catching my eye.
Trees sway in the breeze,
Fireflies dance,
glowing in the moonlight.
The faint hooting of an owl ends
a long silence.

Oliver Cundale (13)
Bishop of Hereford's Bluecoat School

ANGER

I feel so cross, I can't explain
It's burning up inside.
I hope this feeling won't stay
And will soon subside.

I'm getting very angry and grumpy
Nothing is right today.
I feel tired and frumpy
Not forever, I pray.

It's cold, it's raining, and nothing is right
The teachers all look cross.
Maybe they are feeling uptight
But I suppose they are the boss.

Matthew Parrott (12)
Bishop of Hereford's Bluecoat School

WHY ME?

They pulled me down the long alleyway,
Then locked me up,
I knew I hadn't done it,
But why me?
It just isn't fair,
Everyone was silent;
All I could hear were the rats' feet above,
Cold and hungry,
Tired too,
But why me?
I was innocent!

Laura Roberts (12)
Bishop of Hereford's Bluecoat School

WINTER

Like a cold white blanket
Snow covers the lawn.
It comes so quickly.
It's fun and great to play in
But it's there today and gone tomorrow.
The little animals hidden away
Sleeping until the sun comes up -
Robins search for little crumbs
While the squirrels are fast asleep in trees.
Ponds are frozen over
While the ducks search for water.
Children clap their hands
To keep the icy wind out.
Snowmen dotted around the frozen lawn
While dogs dance around them.
Mothers call their children home
As the first snowflakes start to fall.

Claire Howlett (12)
Bishop of Hereford's Bluecoat School

AT THE CIRCUS

C ircular tents where we sit, animals come and go
I nside! Inside! Come on in, is what the ringmaster crows.
R oaring lions, elephants too, *and*
C lowns doing what clowns do.
U nder the tightrope we look up and off
S omebody goes balancing balancing - oh . . .
                              And down they go!

Lorna Webb (12)
Bishop of Hereford's Bluecoat School

LIFE'S A LOTTERY

It's the same every Thursday,
Rushing down the road,
Mum gambles for money,
Wishing for a wealthy load.

First she chooses the digits,
Six of them, one to forty-nine,
Picks them out of a clear glass jar,
Then places them in a line.

And when the 'i'-dotting receptionist,
Hands over the ticket, white and red,
Mum passes over the chunky coin,
Engraved with the Queen's grand head.

Mum returns with the numbered ticket,
Two stubby blue fingers crossed,
She's getting excited about the Lottery,
But I really know she's lost.

Victoria Forster (12)
Bishop of Hereford's Bluecoat School

GRANDPA

Old and frail, sitting in his armchair,
Thinking of his life when he was pure.
His skin, like a gingerbread man,
His eyes' loss of colour waiting to fall into
a deep sleep.
I'm waiting every moment, to see if
I have lost and when the day arrives,
I will know he will always be in my heart.

Charlie Thomas (13)
Bishop of Hereford's Bluecoat School

THE FOREST

The forest was damp and dark.
It was deadly silent apart from the distant rumble of cars.
I walked in a steady, rhythmic pace,
Pausing every now and then to listen for footsteps and voices.
I now started to regret storming off.
The sun dropped lower and lower in the sky.
I felt alone and unloved.
My mind was packed with ideas of what to do.
I then saw in the corner of my eye a disused bench.
It was overrun with spiders and plants.
I decided to take my jumper from around my waist.
I felt tears growing in my eyes I was lost and didn't
                                            know what to do.
When my eyes cleared from the tears it was dusk.
It became cold and I shivered in my big jumper.
I remember getting out of the car for a Sunday walk and
                                    thought how wrong it went.
I just hoped everyone was missing me like I was missing them.
I then heard a rustle. I froze deadly still.
Then, realising it was only an owl I returned to my usual headache.
I just felt alone and unloved.

Ros Moore (12)
Bishop of Hereford's Bluecoat School

MONEY

Money - notes as crisp as lettuce,
Clean and fresh like mints,
When they come from it,
But yet, as they get older,
Their newness starts to fade,
And in its place takes age.

Money - coins as bright as bells,
Their heads gleaming when they're new,
Yet in their old age,
They seem to dullen,
And the smile leaves their face,
And a frown comes in its place.

Neil Phillips (13)
Bishop of Hereford's Bluecoat School

CHOCOLATE!

Chocolate is a wonderful thing.
It can be runny, slimy or just plain solid,
But no way can it be so horrid.
It can be milky or plain, and brown or white
Depending on the kind you like.
It comes in such different shapes and sizes,
From rectangle to triangle, from small to enormous.
Oh what fun, chocolate, you're my life.
Chocolate sponges, chocolate cakes, oh why not
                              chocolate lakes?
Everything should be made of chocolate! Oh chocolate!

My teeth are tightened in a metal cage,
I think it's because of my superior age.
I am always having fillings,
I bet the dentist is making killings.
I know it's sugar, you see
OK, that's less in my tea.
I've suddenly grown gigantic spots.
I tell you, there are lots.
These won't stop me scoffing
Chocolate, the sweet-tooth of life!

Nathan Raine (12)
Bishop of Hereford's Bluecoat School

SUNKEN

You feel your heart sink while you think of the lie you told today.
You feel your heart sink while you think of the children who
aren't able to play.
You feel your heart sink while you think of the people
who feel the need to run away.
You feel your heart sink while you think of the way
you made her get away.
You feel your heart sink while you think of the human race
fading into space.
You feel your heart sink while you think of the money
your mum has to pay.
You feel your heart sink while you think of the people
who slay animals each day.
You feel your heart sink while you think of the love
you get each day.
You feel your heart sink while you think of the people
who can't think so how do they

$$\text{sink}$$
$$\text{away!}$$

Holly Devine (12)
Bishop of Hereford's Bluecoat School

THE CAT

Sitting by the fire curled up tight,
Eyes, two little slits
Fire burns bright.

Fur warm and soft black
As black as night,
Paws stretched out in front
Nose out of sight.

Ears back and forth listening for the sounds,
Alert to its surroundings,
Heartbeats gently pound.

Dying embers in the grate
Coat groomed soft as silk
Empty space by the fireplace
Cat's gone to get her milk.

Ashley Smith (13)
Bishop of Hereford's Bluecoat School

UNITED!

At 3pm it's time to go, time to start the match,
At Old Trafford Newcastle score, instantly it turns quiet.
Fifteen minutes gone, it's still one-nil, to Newcastle of course,
Then United bring on Giggs, Old Trafford starts to roar.

When Giggs gets the ball, you know there's gonna be danger,
As soon as his cross hit Sheringham on the head, we knew
                                        it was a goal!
Goal! Shouts the United crowd. *Boo!* Says Newcastle.
Giggs was the hero, Giggs was the man,
If anyone can do it today, Giggsy can.

So when Giggs went on a run, 2-1 shouted United,
Given went down to dive at his feet, penalty surely?
Referee waves play on, it comes to Cantona,
He shoots, scores, *goal!* . . . United are one up.

At home as I watch TV, the score came in, United had won!

Paul Stewart (12)
Bishop of Hereford's Bluecoat School

SWEETS

Sweets are delicious.
Sweets are sticky.
Sweets are gorgeous.
Sweets are colourful.
Sweets are gooey.
Sweets with filling in them.
Sweets wrapped up in lovely packs.
Sweets put in sparkling jars.

Which sweet would you choose?
Sherbet are my favourite.
Unwrap the wrapper.
Place the shining sweet in your mouth,
Suck the sweet,
Juicy and gooey once you get into the middle,
Sour sweets make you pull a funny face,
As sherbet explodes,
Your mouth trickles.
Sweets!

Vicky Bishop (12)
Bishop of Hereford's Bluecoat School

DOGS

Man's best friend,
Follow you everywhere.
Stay with you until the end.

By night they rummage through the bins,
Looking for some grub,
Then stroll on in,
Looking like they need a scrub.

Coat's shiny and glossy
Big, brown, twinkling eyes,
Look up at you for love and attention.

They think of you as kind,
You think of them as loyal.
You trust them and they will trust you.

Katie Higgins (12)
Bishop of Hereford's Bluecoat School

THE BEAST

Eyes like diamonds,
Glaring,
Staring,
At you.
You know they are there,
Watching you face to face.

Ears like triangles,
Sharp and
Pointed.
The clang of a trash can,
The crying in its run.

In the night sky
With the moonlight on its back
A panther,
Maybe but it's too big,
It must be a cat.

Amy Crowley (12)
Bishop of Hereford's Bluecoat School

A Day Of School Is . . .

School is stressful on Monday mornings,
PSE, RE and maths too.
School is good as well.
Seeing all my friends.
The first lesson starts,
It's maths!
An hour of sheer hell.
Thank God it's break.
I get a doughnut to keep me going
Throughout the next lessons.
After that it's science.
Alleluia, Alleluia it's *lunch.*
Period 4 is geography,
We're learning about Japan,
A very educational lesson.
Last but not least is drama,
One of my best lessons
With no work needed.
I imagine I hear the bell
And people start to pack up.
It's the end of school's first day.
I'm walking home with my mates,
Telling them about my day
With a long sigh.

Matthew Skyrme (12)
Bishop of Hereford's Bluecoat School

SPORT

S port is life
   is conversation
   is communication

P ower, accuracy, strength and stamina.
   There is a sport for everyone

O n the pitch, reputations
   Live or die

R ules enforced by judges, referees, linesmen and
   officials, are rejected or obeyed.

T orment of the crowd keeps the game in good spirit.
   Win or lose, we'll be singing.

Darren Williams (12)
Bishop of Hereford's Bluecoat School

THE LONER

He sits there, huddled in the corner,
Never venturing towards the light.
When the teacher strides over,
He always turns and runs in fright.

In games we all run out to play,
But he stays in and never plays.
At lunch always remains where he is,
He never changes his funny ways.

Then one day we found in horror,
That the loner had left without a trace,
We all then saw some writing there, it said,
This is the *Loner's* place.

Ben Bridgewater (12)
Bishop of Hereford's Bluecoat School

THE SHEEP

The sheep's lovely, thick greyish snugly wool
On the high green hill,
The sun blazing down,
Sheep walking,
The sun beating down,
On the little lamb and his mother as they walk.

What a noise!

The sheep munching at the thick long grass
Walking, hot,
Back down to the big field,
The little sheep's black feet worn down.

What a day!
The little lamb and his mother
Walk into the barn to rest,
After another long day,
Baa.

Jean Chan (12)
Bishop of Hereford's Bluecoat School

CROSS COUNTRY

At the start, everyone pushing and shoving,
Some people sprint, some people walk.

Half way round legs turn to jelly,
Want to stop but have to go on.

Nearly finished, can't stop now!
Try to run faster towards the finish.

Sasha Double (12)
Bishop of Hereford's Bluecoat School

STORM

The Devil roams the sky,
With the wind at his side,
They dance their evil dance,
And guard their territory with pride.

The Devil fires his lightning bolts,
Whilst the wind laughs with glee -
They both watch the clouds groan,
And writhe in agony.

The clouds shed torrential tears,
Which lash down on the Earth,
Devastating all great creation,
Of which the good God gave birth.

The mere mortals are mystified,
As their world is destroyed,
By the wind battles of nature,
Which are impossible to avoid.

The Devil roams the sky,
He succeeded once again.
With help from the wind,
He caused ultimate pain.

But God's golden ball laughs in the sky,
Welcoming the new day -
Laden with fresh hope and happiness,
Driving all sorrow away.

Anne Butterfill (12)
Bishop of Hereford's Bluecoat School

THE FIRE

Fire,
Growing, unstoppable,
Leaping and dancing,
Lighting the world with its cruel glow.
I'm trapped, it's gaining,
Laughing, pumping its sickly smoke into my lungs,
My heart pounds like a thousand drums,
As the intense heat reaches my cringing body.
Sparks flash, my clothes smoulder,
I scream!
But nobody hears.

I crumple to the floor
Can't breathe, see, stand!
Dark clouds drift around the edge of my vision.
But suddenly I hear sounds, voices.
I see people, shouting.
Water sprays everywhere, calming the burning
on my face.
I rejoice!
At least for now,
Fire is dead!

Nick Edmondson (12)
Bishop of Hereford's Bluecoat School

THE COMPUTER MANIAC

He sits at his screen all day long,
I think his brain has been taken over by that CD ROM.
He knows his ROM from his RAM and his RAM from his ROM.
His head's full with so much information
It's ticking like a bomb.

He's on the Internet every day,
Finding more and more info -
He never rests.
One day his mind's gonna blow
Just like a volcano.

Michael Prosser (13)
Bishop of Hereford's Bluecoat School

WEDDINGS - WHAT A FUSS!

Something old, something new,
Something borrowed, something blue.
The glittering white of a wedding dress,
The wrapping paper piled in a mess,
Forgotten in all the confusion,
Best day of your life what an illusion!
Best man, bridesmaids, page boys too,
Maid of honour, someone who?
The bossy mother put to the test,
Will she come out in her Sunday best?
Flowers everywhere, pretty but frail,
Everyone's waiting for the bride to hail.
Here she comes so radiant and calm,
With her father's hand in her palm.
Carefully she steps into the carriage,
That will soon take her to her marriage.
She walks down the aisle drowned in her veil,
With maids following in her trail.
Her mother drops a silent tear,
She wonders how no one hears.
It's all over, they are united as one,
Man and wife they have finally become.

Emma Skinner (14)
Bishop of Hereford's Bluecoat School

LOOKING BACK

As it approaches the midnight hour
I wonder what used to happen
When the slaves worked from dawn 'til dusk
At the old plantation on the edge of town.

The church bells toll for the midnight hour,
As I look at the bright north star.
Then as I look down I noticed two figures as silent as could be.
Neither had a face but one was white,
Well fed and proud.
The other was dark tall and starved,
Then all of a sudden I heard a shriek,
So I looked at the wall again.
The white man had a whip in his hand,
And struck the black man's back.

More slaves seemed to appear,
Standing in lines,
And plants sprouted up,
Which I knew were cotton plants.

Years seemed to drift past,
And then I heard an almighty cheer,
As the slaves seemed to disappear.

Then I suddenly realised
At last the slaves were free.

Emily Mellish (12)
Bishop of Hereford's Bluecoat School

GETTING TO THE MOON

One small step for man, one giant leap for mankind
Is it really that amazing
when you see what else we can find?
The moon is just a tiny molecule floating around space

A giant leap.
More like a pointless flop.
Why don't we just keep
to what we know
until we can dimensions leap?

We wouldn't need to dimensions leap
if we treated our planet with respect.
Look after what we need to keep
                    for humans to survive.

Lewis Morison (12)
Bishop of Hereford's Bluecoat School

HOW WILL WE COPE?

Old John stands waving a white hanky,
It's very emotional to see,
The helpless black nigger,
Children separated from their families
Tears are in their eyes,
Swelling up, then they start
to fall like a calm sad stream.
The happy white house has now disappeared,
Along with old John.
What will happen?
Where will we go?
How will we cope?

Alison Taylor (12)
Bishop of Hereford's Bluecoat School

MY DREAM

My bedroom is like any other
though I have a small blue bedcover.
It sometimes works its way into the hall.
The floor and walls they don't exist.
The floor is covered in a material mist.
The walls are covered in what I call 'bliss'.
Those who I dream to kiss.
My desk is covered in all my junk,
And when my mother saw it her heart just sank.
My brother's bedroom isn't as bad as mine,
He's all good and what my gran calls divine.
He likes the Spice Girls, oh how sad,
When they split up boy will I be glad.

My bedroom is just the way I like it,
a complete and utter tip.

Elizabeth Crabbe 13)
Bishop of Hereford's Bluecoat School

WATER

Water is wet, water is fun,
Water is for everyone,
You drink it, you wash with it,
You can swim in it too,
There's lots of water everywhere,
                    it's for me and for you.
You find it in rivers, in oceans and in lakes,
You can find it relaxing, the gentle sound it makes,
Without it there would be no rain or no snow,
Where would we be without it, I just don't know.

Jacqueline Morgan (12)
Bishop of Hereford's Bluecoat School

COUNTRY MEADOWS

The daisies sprinkled on the ground.
The buttercups look to the sky.
Peace and quiet all around.
Time passing as time goes by.
Little earth hills popping up again,
The moles are quiet burrowing through,
They don't care about the rain,
Slowly, slowly, nothing else to do.
If you're lucky, a rabbit might be seen,
Playing amongst the luscious green.
Night is drawing, another day out,
Time to remember what it's all about.

Jade Griffiths (12)
Bishop of Hereford's Bluecoat School

SMILES

People don't always smile when they are happy!
My sister's smile is often a sly grinny one
and my brother's means he has been naughty!
Mum's smile is make-up all plastered
round her mouth.
Dad's smile is deadly like a saw
cut in two,
But my smile is true I wear
it all the time.
Not only to make others
happy, but to make me
happy too!

Rhianwyn Porter (12)
Bishop of Hereford's Bluecoat School

SNOW

Snowflakes flutter gently to the ground.
Their soft white crystals make silent sounds.
They patter peacefully onto the window-panes,
The only movement in the stillness of the night.

Snow glitters and sparkles in the delicate light of the moon,
Glistening and gleaming as it is bathed in the brightness
                                    of a moonbeam.
It twinkles as the brightness hits its tiny crystal particles,
And scatters the light into one thousand rays of brilliance.

The sky in the east turns from blue, to purple, to a rosy glow
The weak winter sun comes up and shines on the snow.
The golden sunlight reflects off a white unspoilt silky blanket,
The golden sunlight of another perfect day.

Sophie Allen (13)
Bishop of Hereford's Bluecoat School

NO SLEEP

When my mum says
                'Get out of bed'
I mumble to her
            'Wake me up next year.'
                But she says, 'You'll be late, you'll see,
            So if that's what you want,
                Don't listen to me!'

Then she goes away,
                I lie dozing peacefully,
until Dad comes along
                There's no sleep for me!

Jenny Shutt (13)
Bishop of Hereford's Bluecoat School

Looks

Personality,
'Never judge a book by its cover',
In this library of life,
Authors pick and mix.

Personality,
I thought that counts.
So why judge by looks?
It hurts,
each ounce.

Personality,
it's all about beauty.
People comment,
People stare,
Someone sniggers,
eyes glare.

Personality,
that comes second:
No one cares about morality.
The way we are,
we have no say,
but still, we pay.

Personality,
No one cares,
it's just a world of stares.

Iona Stephens (12)
Bishop of Hereford's Bluecoat School

A Tale Of A Conker

As I sit alone in the park
I stare at the conkers shiny and dark
Piles and piles of the beautiful things
The children play and tie them on strings
Then I remember my 67
That's been in my pocket since I was eleven
It's still there, I can feel its shell
Why don't I play, oh what the hell!
I know I'm old but I don't care
I bet I haven't lost the flair!

I sit on the bench and think,
Then I see
A gang of boys come up to me
They laugh and jeer
Smirk and sneer
I turn and head for home, at last.
People laugh as I walk past.
When I get home, I look and see
A sign on my back reading

'Conker-head'

That's me!

Elaine Griffiths (12)
Bishop of Hereford's Bluecoat School

Flight

Wings outstretched,
Humming loud,
Flies through the air
And through the clouds.

Bird of the sky,
Soars into Heaven.
No other bird is like
a *Boeing 747.*

Fiona Storer (13)
Bishop Of Hereford's Bluecoat School

BEEF

It lures you to it
You can't stay away
You have to have it,
every day.
The smell, the texture, the way
that it looks.
There's nothing like it in any book
You can eat it in burgers, sausages too.
But when you eat it like this
you won't hear it moo!
But this wonderful thing that
we adore,
Won't be around anymore.
You see this marvellous creation
comes from a cow
(And before this animal we do bow)
But these creatures will no longer
skip and hop
'Cause soon these cows are off
to the chop.
This amazing creation will no
longer be,
The reason being BSE!

Natasha Loader (12)
Bishop of Hereford's Bluecoat School

LIKE WINTER

Winter arrived,
enveloping the countryside
like a cloud.
The snow fell in spirals,
carpeting the landscape.
The robin arrived,
a brilliant flash of colour,
completing the blank white landscape.
Every tree held icicles
descending
like a series of portcullis.
Spiders' webs hanging
stretched like spun-out silver
decorating every hedgerow.
Trees like skeletons,
brittle and frail
under the blanket.
Everything was perfect,
Like *winter!*

Janet Kay (13)
Bishop of Hereford's Bluecoat School

GUILTY CONSCIENCE

We did a bad thing today,
me and my best mate.
Something we will always regret,
but others might not forgive and forget.

If only we could turn back time,
we wouldn't have done this terrible crime.
The whole of the school seems to know.
We don't know what to do or where to go.

People point and people stare,
we're fed-up of having to act
as though we just don't care.

We feel guilty, we feel shame,
people would understand if they'd done the same.
All we seem to do is hide,
nobody we know is on our side.

Charlotte Hughes (13)
Bishop of Hereford's Bluecoat School

GERMS V DISINFECTANT!

We are the germs, we will win,
We hang around the toilet, the sewers and the bin.
We strive to make your teeth decay,
In every dirty, selfish way.

We hang out behind a dirty toenail,
Sweaty feet - they never fail!
We feed on limbs pulsating with pus,
Anything grubby, we don't make a fuss!

We are the disinfectants, the soaps and
the bleaches,
We're so clean, we smell of peaches!
We're sure to win, we're healthy and clean,
The slobby germs - they are so mean.

Here we come with our laser guns set,
If we don't get you soon, we'll get you yet!
The match is soon - we're ready for the kill,
When we've finished with you, you will be *ill*!

Sarah Clelland (13)
Bishop of Hereford's Bluecoat School

WORLD DESTRUCTION

As the trees fall,
there's a thump on the ground.
A tear comes to my eye
with every sound.
Soon the trees will no longer be there,
the countryside will be bare.
The houses are taking over,
every inch of our land.
In my opinion,
it should be banned.
The human race takes over,
soon there will be nothing left,
but the buzz of cars and lorries,
whilst doing the deed of theft.

Hannah May Davis (13)
Bishop of Hereford's Bluecoat School

LOVE

Love can turn you upside down,
Turn your emotions round and round.
People told me to stay away,
Told me you were just out to play.
I never knew I could hurt like this,
I thought you loved me,
I thought I'd found bliss.
I'll never forget the first embrace,
Or the way, you touched my face.
And now you've gone I know I'll miss
Your warm, tender, loving kiss.
But now you've left me now I know
That all your love was just a show.

Emily Burrow (13)
Bishop of Hereford's Bluecoat School

THE SECRET LOVE

As they pass each other during school,
She smiles sweetly.

Her friends ask her who he is,
'Nobody,' she replies.
Somehow they know she is lying.

In the dinner queue
They don't say a word.
But the way he leans is so perfect.

They meet again during science,
He says 'Hi,'
Her heart melts.

As soon as the bell rings,
He is soon gone.

She walks home, alone,
Left with her thoughts.

Lucy Maslen (13)
Bishop of Hereford's Bluecoat School

FIRE AND MAN

Alive and hot, starts with a spark,
Glowing red in the dark.
Colours flaming, red, green or yellow,
Lack of air will make it mellow.
Fire fed little or not shielded carefully,
Will diminish and die, or grow wild and free.
Even so, without love, care or attention,
Man grows wild without redemption.

Francis Hewitt (12)
Bishop of Hereford's Bluecoat School

SO-CALLED FRIENDS!

I was sitting in science on a boring day,
I changed my friends now it's time to pay,
I thought they were all my friends,
But now I know I was mistaken.

They sent a letter round the class,
I don't know how long it's going to last.
They aren't my friends I don't know why,
I try to look happy and not to cry.

I thought these friends were going to last
But now that thought is in the past.
I want us all to be just mates,
I think that it must be just fate.

They talk about me behind my back.
I just want to cover my head with a sack.
I tell them all I feel fine.
I don't want to mope about and whine.

Zoe Warren (13)
Bishop of Hereford's Bluecoat School

THE DAY OF A SLAVE

The working day is over and the slaves are going in.
They will have what little food the white men give.
They go into the cabin on to the hard dirt floor.
Their black and white bodies drop to the floor like rags.
The slaves are huddled tightly together trying to sleep.
But before they know it the working bell is ringing,
                                   time for another day!

Sam Turner (12)
Bishop of Hereford's Bluecoat School

SOMBRE AWAKENING

Slowly, we marched all night in the rain,
Bullets, barbed wire, terror, pain,
Blankets of gas creep through,
Taking a toll of lost hopes that nobody knew.

An eruption of fire bursts across,
On gaunt, splintered landscape claims loss,
From the state of life to inert,
It seems pointless to stay alert.

Yet again the horizon lights up,
Through acrid, yellow haze.
Pin-pointed men,
This lottery will sort out the maze.

Why are we here?
Have we lost God's ear?

Oliver Partridge (14)
Bishop of Hereford's Bluecoat School

SIX FOOT DEEP

In the fields by day
On the straw by night
In the fields picking cotton.
Helping one another
Trying not to get whipped
Trying to stay on our feet
Even though we're tired and weak.
Living on scraps and wheat
Trying not to sink six foot deep.

Jacob Greasley (12)
Bishop of Hereford's Bluecoat School

IMAGINATION

You wake up in the night,
all you can see are weird shapes and blurry shadows.
You look down,
the carpet could be moving but you're not sure.
You quickly turn to see this towering shape looking over you,
is it your wardrobe or not?
You think you see something moving on the far side of the room,
what could it be?
A beam of light shines through the curtains highlighting one wall.
Black dots scatter one area,
are they spiders, or is it your
imagination?

Ben Stephens (14)
Bishop of Hereford's Bluecoat School

BULLYING

She follows me around everywhere,
Then she gives an evil stare.
I walk to my class like I always do,
With her right behind me,
Not knowing what she's going to do.
We get into the classroom and I sit down,
As she gives me an ugly frown.
But I ignore her and do my work,
While she is doodling on the back of my shirt.
I can never wait till the end of school,
After all she cannot follow me,
And make me look like a fool.

Vicky Phillips (13)
Bishop Of Hereford's Bluecoat School

HIS MISTAKE

He's made a lot of mistakes
In his time
But never one like this.
He's tripped over the cat
So bought a dog. That's a mistake!

He's made a lot of mistakes
In his time
But never one like this.
He's been bitten by the mouse,
So bought a rat. That's a mistake!

He's made a lot of mistakes
In his time
But never one like this.
His sister killed herself,
So he killed his brother. That's a *mistake!*

He's made a lot of mistakes
In his time,
But this one's the best,
He's had so many mistakes,
He's killed himself! That's a good mistake!

Phew! That's the end of his mistakes,
Unless he's got a son!
He really had a lot of mistakes
In his life
But now they are all over!

Malcolm Rogers (12)
Bishop of Hereford's Bluecoat School

GOING FOR GOAL

He steps up,
Places the smooth rounded sphere on
the white paint mark,
The noise of millions of people roaring
in his ears,
He takes three steps back and one step
to the side,
He sees the large round figure
surrounded by a big white framework,
He begins to run,
Lifts his right leg up a little then
quickly swings it forward, the ball flies
off the ground and into the back of the net.

Goal!

Matt Watkins (12)
Bishop of Hereford's Bluecoat School

THE FUNERAL

The sound of the silence,
Beats upon your ears,
It surrounds you like a fog and fills you,
Smothering you,
Paralysing you.
And then it is
Broken,
By the cry of a single human being,
Caught up with the emotion of the moment,
Their wails fill the air,
Ripping through the calm, and suddenly,
The storm breaks.

Julia Reese (13)
Bishop of Hereford's Bluecoat School

TO BE FREE

*(Written in the view of an American
Slave in the 1800's)*

At harvest time each year
We have to work long hours
Sixteen hours each day
To harvest all the cotton.

Oh how I'd love to be free
Away from this hard labour
I'd follow the 'drinking gourd'
To Canada the promised land.

If we go wrong and break the rules
We have the whip on our back
The cat o'nine tails with nine whips in one
Is very painful and hard.

Oh how I'd like to be free
Away from loads of whippings
I'd follow the 'drinking gourd'
To Canada the promised land.

If I escaped I would head to
Canada where it is free
The black people there have equal rights
Not like us old 'niggers'.

Oh how I'd like to be free
In Canada with equal rights
I'll follow the 'drinking gourd'
To Canada the promised land.

Adam Wright (12)
Bishop of Hereford's Bluecoat School

SHADOWS AT NIGHT

It stalks you all day
Stealing your body
Sticking to you like glue
Until the sun goes down
Putting an end to its torment
As it disappears
Or does it?

The darkness closes in
As you walk home from work
Down the dark alleyway
Something is watching you
Waiting to pounce
You walk past a lamppost and there it is
The beastly black form
You call your shadow
'The silent stalker of the night'.

Carl Lappin (13)
Bishop of Hereford's Bluecoat School

THE TRACTOR!

The key turns in the ignition,
The tractor moves position,
The engine roars,
And the smoke pours.

The tractor moves into the field,
It slips and slides but never stops,
It comes to a puddle, the water splashes,
But the tractor never stops.

The rain pours down,
But it ploughs through the mud,
The lights light it up like a clown,
But the tractor comes to a halt.

The driver looks to see what's wrong,
But it just stands like an elephant,
The key's turned again,
And it roars like a lion.

David Stuffins (13)
Bishop Of Hereford's Bluecoat School

ARACHNAPHOBIA

Dark shadows in the corner of the room.
Dust? Eyes blink to bring the shape into view.
A closer inspection is required.
Instead I pull the covers over my head
shuddering, hot and sweating.
Lying low in my lair,
just the beat of my heart, thundering in my ear.
Gradually I pluck up courage and
blink again out into the stark, bright light.

A slight movement along the wall tells me it's my worst fear.
Long thin angular bony legs scuttle downwards towards me.
My body, paralysed, screams out silently.

Daisy Gell (13)
Bishop Of Hereford's Bluecoat School

LONELY OLD ME

I'm just an ordinary bloke
There's nothing wrong with me
But 'cause I ain't got any friends,
I've spent me life at sea.

I've got fishes in the cargo box,
And lobsters on the brain
My cabin reeks with strong sea smells,
And limpets hog my anchor chain.

The porpoises ignore me
When I honk a friendly warning
I think they think that I am mad
To get up early every morning.

The sharks are something I avoid
They give a nasty bite
But I know when they're in my net,
'Cause boy, they sure ain't light.

The dolphins keep me company
On many starry nights
We sing in perfect harmony
Until the sun is shining bright.

The one thing that I really miss
Is talking with a mate,
Though having to be sociable,
Is something that I hate.

I still feel very lonely
Perhaps one day I'll head for home,
But then I'll just be turned away
A victim to the sea of foam.

No, I think I'm destined to be out here,
Out among the waves of emptiness.

Emma Hagger (12)
Bishop of Hereford's Bluecoat School

SCHOOL

School is cruel!
I hate most lessons especially maths.
All the adding and dividing,
Teachers shouting
'Cos we're talking.

School is boring!
Lunchtime, detentions, demerits, litter duty
                        and much much more.

School is cool!
At half-past three
That's when we get out of this horrible dump.
Some catch buses, some just walk
But I have to stay till 4.30.

School is okay
In the end!
Some teachers are okay, I suppose.
Some give you house points,
Some give you merits
But the worst thing is you
        have to go again tomorrow.

Chloe Lyons (12)
Bishop of Hereford's Bluecoat School

BAD FAMILY

Grown-ups are ogres,
Grown-ups are beasts,
Grown-ups always get to have feasts,
While I have to go to bed early not late.

Babies gurgle,
Babies can't talk,
Babies get carried, they don't have to walk,
They get all the attention.

Toddlers are awful,
Toddlers are tykes,
Toddlers have extra wheels on their bikes,
They never get the blame.

Kids go to school,
Kids love sweets,
Kids can't put shoes on their feet,
They're always innocent (to grown-ups).

Grandparents are boring,
Grandparents moan,
Grandparents get pensions, a bit of a loan,
They get everything done for them.

Teenagers are amazing,
Teenagers are cool,
Teenagers get homework, we work enough at school,
It's a hard life.

Matthew Mottram (12)
Bishop of Hereford's Bluecoat School

A Dog Called Ben And His Go-Kart

Four o'clock I'm home
Come on Ben, come on Ben
No time for a comb.
Where is he, it's time to go
Start the go-kart, no need for a tow.

The thrill of speed with Ben
In need of a good race
Against the go-kart.
Over the bumps and over the hills
Most of the time on two fat wheels.

With only a tongue with
Which to sweat,
Ben jumps into the pond
To get cool and wet.

Rick Cleland (12)
Bishop of Hereford's Bluecoat School

Sweets

Sweets are sticky and lush.
They stick to your teeth and make them drop out,
The shelves are piled as high as the clouds.
Everlasting gob-stoppers . . .
So big they fill your mouth.
Marshmallows, chocolate bars, cakes,
Sherbet lemons, sherbet dips, *ahh . . . !*
I think I'm in heaven.

Craig Shaw (12)
Bishop of Hereford's Bluecoat School

HOCKEY

We are going
to win.
the opposition
are wimps.
Grazing of
knees.
Tumbling over.
One glorious
goal.
Hooray!
Attacking to
get the ball.
We've got the
ball now!
Defending the
goal.

Half-time!

Two goals
Go on Bishops
We can win.

Bang!

Another goal.
They are too
easy to beat!

We win, ha ha!
You lose
I'm not surprised.

Hannah Barter (12)
Bishop of Hereford's Bluecoat School

BONFIRE NIGHT

A small crackle,
and a spurt of flames.
The first twig lights.
Gently, blue flames surge up the next twig.
And the next, and the next.
The recurring flicker and spit.
Last year's three-piece suite,
up in flames.
A small gasoline can explodes.
The orange glow explores,
finds a lover and stays.
The flames lick higher and higher,
Surging gently,
Upwards.
Half-way.
There's no stopping yet.
A flash, and the Christmas tree is gone
forever.
The sweet smell of wood chip,
from before you concreted the patio.
The black, charcoal twigs,
snap rhythmically.
Guy Fawkes is engulfed by the flames.
The face is last to go.
Black, coal eyes, staring back,
Calling.
The flames die down.
All is lost.

Rebeccah Wadeson (13)
Bishop Of Hereford's Bluecoat School

SUFFERING . . .

The suffering struck at a premature age.
I'd lost my freedom, got trapped in a cage.
Pain and upset got me down,
My childhood smiles turned to angry frowns.
I got sent to a place that nobody knew of,
The days spent surrounded by shallow love,
On the surface there was slight care,
It got to a stage that I could not bear.
Of those nurses paid to do a mother's job,
On the bed I would deeply sob.
Missing life and friends at home,
Around the ward I would miserably roam,
Normality was too much to ask,
A game of netball became a task.
Could no one save this young soul of mine?
Maybe it just took all that time.
Many years we've spent with chronic fatigue,
An energetic life was clearly out of my league.

Sophie Hewitt (13)
Bishop Of Hereford's Bluecoat School

I AM A SLAVE

I am a slave
Sad and scared
I am a slave
Hardworking and starved.

I am a slave
Hungry and tired
I am a slave
Small and used.

I am a slave
Frightened and lonely.
I am a slave
Crippled and in pain.

I am a slave
Who plucks the cotton
I am a slave
A 'nigger folk'.

Ben Carter (13)
Bishop of Hereford's Bluecoat School

LIFE

Why is life so cruel,
When you've always acted the fool?
When someone you love, dearly,
Are very close, nearly
To the end.
You feel sorrow,
You feel pain,
Any more mixed emotions,
And you think you'll go insane.
But at the end of the tunnel,
There's light,
Just enough to see, it's in sight
One more step,
And you can have it,
Then the pain will go away,
And the love will stay,
And never go away.

Zöe Cruse (14)
Bishop Of Hereford's Bluecoat School

THE CHEETAH

Sharp eyes always watching,
Moving silently in the grass,
Cautiously waiting, waiting,
Suddenly! Opportunity comes at last.

The chase begins,
His lean sleek body,
Moves like the wind,
The cheetah wins,
His prey succumbs.

He is satisfied,
He eats his prey alone,
All the other animals have scattered,
Leaving the hunter to his prey.

Laura Jefferies (13)
Bishop of Hereford's Bluecoat School

ANGEL DELIGHT

The smooth, shiny bodywork lay dormant.
The tall, silver choppers were still.
Suddenly, a brown, hairy hand gripped the bodywork.
The machine rose high into the air.
The silver choppers swirled violently.
Then!
The machine plummeted into a pink, frothy liquid.
The choppers spun, the liquid bubbled.
The machine is removed, the choppers halted.
There you have it,
Angel Delight!

Peter Owen (14)
Bishop Of Hereford's Bluecoat School

LOVE

Looking at him across the room,
Feeling warm inside when he turns and smiles,
His seems to go on for miles.
Bright white teeth shining through,
Sparkling and glistening in the light
breaking through.
Chilly breeze on the back of your
neck,
Goose-bumps creeping down your legs.
People enter breaking the trance.
Hoping he looks back just by
chance.

Walking over to talk to him,
Not knowing what to say.
Standing there in silence,
Should you say it, maybe not.
Muttering words that don't make sense,
Making yourself feel even more tense.
Walking away nothing said,
Only wishing that you were dead.

Giving up seems the best,
Walking away to have a rest.
Calling you back, you turn and run,
Just like a bullet out of a gun.
Now no problems with your words,
All you can say is 'Thank you Lord!'

Joanne Lambourne (14)
Bishop Of Hereford's Bluecoat School

THE FOUR SEASONS

Spring,
Plants have started to bud,
Animals begin to stir,
The early morning chorus starts,
The scenery starts to form.

Summer,
Flowers are blooming,
Animals awake,
The colours shoot out from all directions,
The scenery is made.

Autumn,
The flowers are closing,
The animals curl up,
The dullness comes back out again,
A tremendous change is made.

Winter,
All the life has gone,
The animals have hidden,
Jack Frost has only just arrived,
This is time for riddance.

Anne-Marie Easdale (14)
Bishop Of Hereford's Bluecoat School

MY FEELING INSIDE

What do you feel? How do you feel?
What do any of us feel inside?
Are we happy? Are we hurting?
Is it pain? Is it strength?
Is it power? Is it weakness?
Can we estimate our innermost feeling . . . ?
Can we cope?

Strangely we achieve more good from hope,
Is there really a need for hope
Or are we just insecure?
We are also scared.
We need a part of certainty,
Something we can depend on.
Something we can trust.

Nathaniel Bishop (12)
Bishop of Hereford's Bluecoat School

THE KIDNAPPING

Late last night when the clock struck ten,
From the sky fell four green men.
I invited them in and they all had tea,
Then said they'd come to kidnap me.
I said I couldn't come today
Because my mum had gone away.
My dad was out as was my brother,
So please could they take up another.
'That's OK,' I heard one say,
'I'm sure we'll find
Another kind
To take on a trip
In our little space ship.'
So off they went
With their long necks bent
To go and see
Who it would be.

So if these aliens visit you,
You'll know exactly what to do.
Just tell them that the time's not right
            and to come again another night.

Natalie Gladwin (13)
Bishop Of Hereford's Bluecoat School

NOISE

I like noise

The zap of a laser gun, the crash in a mine.
The splash of a fish at the end of the line.

The ticking sound of a clock as time goes by,
The trickling sound of water in the River Wye.

The creaking sound of an old rusty door.
The sound of bottles being smashed against a wall.

The splashing sound of a massive whale.
The whistling sound of a really big gale.

The roar of a plane, the buzz of a fly.
The cackle of witches flying high in the sky.

The whirling of a whirlpool as it goes round and round.
The pitter patter of rain as it hits the ground.

The monotonous tone of a boring old teacher.
The singing sound of a fairly young preacher.

The hiss of a cat as it sees a dog.
The squeak of some mice, the croak of a frog.

I like noise.

Adam Westlake (13)
Bishop Of Hereford's Bluecoat School

THE HEDGEHOG

As you look
Deep into the forest.
Past the fences.
Through the trees.
Past the opening
Into the autumn leaves,
The slow movement begins.

The leaves begin to move.
An opening appears.
A nose shuffles its way through,
A head appears,
Two front feet,
A spiky body,
And finally, two back feet.

The hedgehog slowly shuffles along,
Nose in the air.
The smell of autumn
In the strong autumn breeze.

The hedgehog turns his nose,
Waddles back to his home,
Burrows his way into the leaves.
The hedgehog
Sleeps once more.

Emma Turner (13)
Bishop Of Hereford's Bluecoat School

A POEM ABOUT FRIENDS

Friends are around to have a laugh with,
To tell secrets that you know they'll keep.
To tell you when your make-up's all wonky,
Or when your hair isn't quite going right.
To sit with and pour over good-looking boys,
Or talk for hours about shoes and clothes.
To share the same interests like music and sports
And to watch favourite TV shows with.
To be there when you need cheering up at times
When things aren't quite going right,
And to share in your laughter and join in your fun
When you're feeling on top of the world!

Friends are like sunrises; beautiful and bright,
Lightening up your day!

Victoria Seaman (13)
Bishop Of Hereford's Bluecoat School

THE MOUSE

Scraping and scratching in the dark,
Under the cupboard, the mouse lives.
Avoiding the traps and poison for him,
He chews on the wood for all of the day.
The day has come, he knew it would,
When he eats the poison and scratches no more.

Matthew Watkins (13)
Bishop Of Hereford's Bluecoat School

HAIR . . .

Lies flat on your head or a bushy mess
Some people want more,
Some people want less.
Shiny and soft or greasy and slimy
Tied up high or pulled back in a bun
Spiky, curly, long and furry
Washed every day gets greasy
Washed once a week still gets greasy
Some people have blonde, some black
Then there's brown
Red, of course, and watch that force
Some call it silver, some call it grey
But there's no getting away
You get older every day.

Anna Jones (14)
Bishop Of Hereford's Bluecoat School

THE JUNK ROOM

Memories smothered in dust.
Cobwebs shroud in unforgetting mist.
Lives lay at rest
In this grave of silence.
Cradle, empty lies,
A crumpled silk doll
Remembers stories of lost lives.

Sophie Rowberry (13)
Bishop Of Hereford's Bluecoat School

SLAVERY

S ilence not a sound, except for the footsteps
  of the Masai,

L ong time I have been here,

A ngry sad and lonely,

V ery hard I toiled all day long,

E very day the sun beats down burning my
  back,

R ain, not a single drop, on the parched
  land

Y earning to escape and break free.

Sian Morris (12)
Bishop Of Hereford's Bluecoat School

BENJI

He walks gracefully,
Eats greedily,
Hunts silently,
Sleeps peacefully,
Purrs contentedly,
And miaows hopefully.
After all,
He is a *cat!*

Rebeka Ellam (13)
Bishop Of Hereford's Bluecoat School

AUTUMN DAYS

Leaves falling, slowly, slowly,
Squirrels hurriedly making their nests.
I like summer, winter and spring,
But very clearly autumn's the best!

It's not too hot, it's not too cold,
The wind is gently blowing,
Animals start to hibernate,
Into their nests they're going!

Look around you, what can you see?
Brown, orange and red.
As the leaves fall off the trees,
They make a colourful bed.

Ellie Southall (11)
Burlish Middle School

WINTER

The snow swirls round
I know I'm going to play
It hits the ground
Oh, what a beautiful day.

I open my door
To be hit for sure
It's cold outside
But I'm going for a sledge ride.

Now it's all over
The night is here
It's silent in Dover
The snow is quite near.

Louise Broadley (11)
Burlish Middle School

THE WITCHING HOUR

Have you ever awoken in the middle of the night,
Frozen with fright?
Have you ever awoken in the witching hour?
When it feels likes you're the only one in the world awake
And looked out through your window
Onto the dark deserted streets below
And it feels like someone's watching.
As you look at the houses in the street
You wonder why there are moonbeam shadows
Cast on their walls,
When there's nobody there to cast them.
When it's so silent,
So still,
That you're afraid to make a sound.
So silent,
So still,
Except for the whistling breeze
That creeps underneath your bedroom door,
That sends an icy shiver up your spine
And chills your toes
Like icicles.

Emma Rainsford (12)
Burlish Middle School

AUTUMN

Walking quietly through the trees,
Crunching gently on the falling leaves,
The colours changing with each day,
Making a carpet to pave my way,
The autumn wind's now getting strong,
More leaves fall as you walk along.

The woodland looks a pretty sight,
With all the colours oh so bright,
I wonder why all things must change,
But that's for another day to arrange.

Sarah Smith (11)
Burlish Middle School

THE SEASONS

The air is cool and breezy,
Flowers sway in the wind,
The sun is shining brightly,
Warm upon my face,
Making my cheeks glow.

Crystal clear snow glistens on the cool ground,
Little red noses all around,
The smell of Christmas turkey drifts from chimneys,
Children start laughing, joyfully,
Opening their Christmas gifts,
Such a joyful time of the year.

Leaves crunch beneath my feet,
All the colours of the world, yellow, green, red, brown,
Children throwing leaves into the breezy air,
Letting them drift through the air,
Chimneys smoking.

Sun is shining so brightly,
Children eating ice-pops,
People in the pool,
Cooling down,
Waiting, waiting, for summer to end.

Gemma Shaw (11)
Burlish Middle School

AUTUMN

Autumn, autumn,
leaves falling
to the ground,
feel that
cool breeze
cold days
cool nights
see those
falling leaves.
Hear those
conker shells
bouncing on the ground.
Smell that fresh rain
after a shower.
Sense that
children are having
a good time
with the conkers.

Luke Martin (11)
Burlish Middle School

AUTUMN

Autumn falls . . .
Days are shorter, nights are longer.
Trees are clothed in browns and red.
Surrounded by a patchwork carpet
Slowly, slowly leaves begin to fall
Until trees bear no leaves at all.
Suddenly, winter is upon us,
Stark trees in a snow-swept world.

Lauren Bucceri (12)
Burlish Middle School

MY AUTUMN POEM

Autumn, autumn everywhere,
Autumn, autumn in the air,
Autumn, autumn is the best,
Don't forget to wear your vest.

Autumn, autumn in the air,
Autumn, autumn choose carefully what you wear,
Autumn, autumn it is nice,
Look, I can see harvest mice.

Autumn, autumn everywhere,
Autumn, autumn you could eat a pear,
Autumn, autumn the nights are dark,
Listen I can hear a dog bark.

Mark Harrodine (11)
Burlish Middle School

THE BIRD

Flying gently through the air
with acrobatic twirls,
Gliding swiftly through the air
with many dancing whirls.

Moving, darting through the air
high above the trees,
Whizzing quickly through the air
flowing with the breeze.

Speeding, swooping through the air
what a wonderful place to be,
Floating, drifting through the air,
How I wish that it was me!

Rachel Pitman (11)
Burlish Middle School

BONFIRE NIGHT

I hear a bang up
in the sky, I look up
high to see a twirling
Catherine wheel, floating
high up in the sky.
I see the smoke drift away
I hear some crackling at
the log fire - there are flames
going everywhere.

The night is cold, there are
colours in the air. The fire is
warm and so is my hair,
it's a nice crisp night
and the mice just fight.

The ants are warm from
the fire. There's a dummy in there.
The dummy is almost gone
from the blazing flame. It's an
amazing thing to watch
especially the biggest one.

Bradlie Bucceri (11)
Burlish Middle School

HALLOWE'EN

Children running up the streets,
We hear the patter of their feet,
We hear them knock the door and sing,
With all the strange unearthly things.

Sarah Taylor (12)
Burlish Middle School

BONFIRE NIGHT

Swirling, curling, whizzing, fizzing,
reds, greens, whites and blues
light up the sky.
Fly, fly my friends in the dark
night's sky.

Bang, boom, crackle, pop.
Scarves, jumpers, nice warm top.
Fire, smoke, ash, *boom, bang, bash*,
sparklers writing names.

Warm near the fire,
damp, cold grass.
Crash! There goes another one.

Swirl, twirl, red, pinks, oranges.
Fireworks are my
favourite things.
There goes another one.
Boom, bang, crash.
But beware take care!

Scott Bentley (11)
Burlish Middle School

A CLEAR DAY

The sky was clear,
The sun was bright,
No cloud to be seen in sight,
I spied a bird, soaring high in the sky,
He swooped down low,
Then widdled in my eye.

Philip Baldwin (12)
Burlish Middle School

AUTUMN DAYS

Autumn days when the grass is jewelled
Matches put off by a snowy pitch
Cold, frost, wind and snow, the sort of weather of autumn,
Flood by the river because of all the rain.

Conker matches going on,
Bits flying in the air,
Smash, bang, wallop, crack.
Conker's come off the string so stamp on it.
Crash, bang, wallop.
I just beat you.

Fluttering, twirling, swirling, curling, falling
On the hard grass floor.
Stamp on them.
Hear them crisp, crunch and crackle.
Red, yellow, orange, rusty gold, brown and purple.
The different colours of the leaves.

Robert Phillips (11)
Burlish Middle School

SPORTS DIVISION

Sports Division is the store,
Where you get the right score.

Fila and Nike are the names you want to get,
Down with the crowd is the best bet.

Don't take a chance don't try anywhere else,
Go to Sports Division where there's no doubt.

David Ireland (12)
Burlish Middle School

As Soon As I Get Home From School

As soon as I get home from school,
I sit on the settee,
I like to sit for hours and hours,
watching the TV.

As soon as I get home from school,
I want something to eat,
I like to eat for hours and hours,
watching the TV.

But when I get home from school,
my mum always says to me,
'I'd like you to do your homework please,
before you watch TV.'

Andrew Butler (11)
Burlish Middle School

What Am I?

I am the bird that flies above,
I am the flower, white as a dove,
I am the stream flowing down,
I am a rabbit, fluffy and brown,
I am a hamster running around,
I am the ear that hears the sound,
I am a fire burning hot,
I am a broken clock, with no tick-tock,
I am wind that can blow,
I am a snail walking slow,
I am a small trickle of blood,
I am a big wet patch of mud.
What am I?

Sadie Tandy (12)
Burlish Middle School

THE CAT

His long dark fur,
his big black eyes,
he often takes
me by surprise.

He likes to sit
upon my lap,
and have a
peaceful cat-nap.

One day he was all alone,
lying in the burning sun,
but then came a butterfly,
and he had found some fun.

Then he gets tired,
so he goes home to bed,
his favourite place to sleep,
is at the top of my head.

Charlotte Harris (11)
Burlish Middle School

I HAVE FAT JUICY SALMON ALL FOR TEA

I live in Jamaica
By the deep blue sea;
I have fat juicy salmon
All for tea
Big ones, small ones
I take my pick;
If I eat too much
I'll be sick.

Craig Johnstone (11)
Burlish Middle School

MY WISH

I have a wish,
About my favourite thing, horses.
This is my wish,

To get a horse,
To muck it out,
To ride it round the moors.

My destiny is to ride a race,
Or jump a jumping course,
What life would be with my horse.

Gymkhanas, races, jumping,
These are all my dreams.

If only these would all come true,
My life would be great.
I have passion for my wish,
And I hope it will happen soon.

Martha Clingan (11)
Burlish Middle School

MIDSUMMER SUN

Autumn is the golden leaves,
Falling from the battered trees,
The violent wind is blowing cold,
A field left alone,
With no one to make it home sweet home,
But what joy it will bring at summertime,
When girls and boys have great fun,
In the midsummer sun.

Natasha Beddard (11)
Burlish Middle School

PEACEFUL HARMONY

Stepping daintily over hot sand,
Trying not to burn my feet.
Leaping down to the sea,
Feeling the ice-cold water
Splashing at my feet.

Walking along the shore,
Rummaging my feet through the damp sand.
The beach peaceful and deserted,
The only sound is a gull on the cliff edge.

Yet I know that in a few hours' time,
There will be a lot of hustle and bustle,
So I observe the peacefulness,
As I watch the orangey sun
Take its place in the sky.

Cheryl Adams (12)
Burlish Middle School

LESSONS

Maths, English and science,
Who could ask for more?
With an art room and a science lab,
There's a lesson behind each door.

Books, books and more books,
With homework every night,
I can hardly look,
Because it gives me such a fright.

Claire Williams (11)
Burlish Middle School

THE PICNIC!

We brought a rug to sit on,
our lunch was in a tin.
We also brought a plastic bag,
to put the rubbish in.

> My brother and my sister,
> made an awful mess.
> My sister spilt her orange juice,
> all over her new dress.

'You silly girl' my mother cried,
'I told you not to wear it.'
'Never mind,' my father said
'I guess that we can spare it.'

> The picnic was all over,
> time to go back home.
> The others were still arguing,
> so I went back on my own.

Emily Hobson (11)
Burlish Middle School

THE POWERFUL SEA

The sea crashes against the shore,
Destroying everything in its path.
The sea creatures wait
In anguish
For the end.
The sky is dark,
The wind howls,
The raging sea never calms.
Will it ever?

Laura Southall (12)
Burlish Middle School

SCHOOL LIFE

'Miss, Jane said I'm a horrible singer
Miss, Henry just trod on my finger.
Miss, can I go to the loo?'
'No you can't you've got too much work to do!'

Wow, I've never heard her shout like that before!
'Get on with your work! Shut that door!'
'Miss I feel ill.'
'Go and bring me a headache pill.'
(Said the teacher).

'There's ink on the floor, get it up,
Everyone shut up,
And stop.'
Hip hip hooray, it's the end of the day.

'Tidy up, go to your locker.
Sarah's running, someone stop her.
Everyone go home, I've had enough,
Thank goodness tomorrow's Saturday,
School life's tough.'

Melissa Pearson (11)
Burlish Middle School

SEA

The sea
is blue
from top to bottom,
With glistening
sparkles from
the sun.

Natasha Noyes (12)
Burlish Middle School

TORNADOES

Twisting, turning to and fro
Nobody does know why
The tornado dives and flies
Through the cloudy skies.

It's a mystery why the tornado seeks to kill
Sweeping nature off the hills
The trees die
Because of the way this monster flies.

The world cries as it goes through the skies
Pulling houses off the ground.
This monster circles round and round
Risking all of our lives.

Joanne Portman (11)
Burlish Middle School

HIGH MOON

The blue, the very dark blue sky,
      With
The moon, the moon dancing up so high,
      With
The grey, the grey holes on the sphere,
      With
The gloomy, the gloomy shadows all over,
      Oh
The moon is in the sky . . .

        . . . but why?

Julie Longmore (11)
Burlish Middle School

AUTUMN

Autumn is here,
Can't you tell?
It's cold and wet,
Like a wintry spell.
Leaves turning yellow,
From green to brown.
The wind and the rain
Are bringing them down.
The days are short,
The nights are long,
The birds no longer
Sing their songs.
People walking along the street,
Kick the leaves up with their feet.
Autumn come winter . . . it's bleak.

Melissa Kennedy (11)
Burlish Middle School

THE LOST SEA

I hear the sea
crashing against the rocks.
The roaring waves in a rage of fury.
Mist gathered,
but the waves rid the gloom of the grey sky.
Seagulls in the sky, circling,
Then suddenly the scene before me,
was engulfed by a billow of smoke
and was lost forever.

Kerri Duce (12)
Burlish Middle School

THE WATERFALL

Crashing, roaring,
Tumbling, falling,
Down, down, down and away,
All the night and all the day.

Along the top,
And over the rocks,
It is wide, it is tall,
This is the day of the waterfall.

The river is
Swishing, turning,
And the hot sun is burning,
Then suddenly, the water's falling.

The water's falling,
And the birds are calling,
It is wide, it is tall,
This is the way of the waterfall.

Laura K Hobbs (11)
Burlish Middle School

UPON THE SEA

Upon the sea
we swiftly move
from edge to edge
through and through
rocking around
on the ocean waves
up and down
like a stave.

Sam Hibbert (12)
Burlish Middle School

I'm Going To See The Sea

I'm going to see the sea,
And have ice-cream for tea.
Where ships have sailed and sank,
I'm living a memory.

Oh my life was changed forever,
When I lost my husband Trevor,
Those happy memories broken,
By that horrible, nasty weather.

When I think of the time I spent,
With that perfect sailor gent.
When we went there together,
I'd just love to know where he went.

Legend says he was drowned at sea,
If he wasn't - where can he be?
When I look through our photos I think,
That he went on that voyage for me.

So I'm going to see the sea,
And have ice-cream for tea,
Where ships have sailed and sank
I'm living a memory.

Phillipa Smith (12)
Burlish Middle School

Autumn

The leaves are falling,
autumn is here;
summer has gone
winter is near.

The wind is blowing,
and the days are shortening;
we will soon smell bonfires burning
the snow will come soon enough.

Max Westwood (12)
Burlish Middle School

MY LIFE

My life is boring,
Every day I'm dawdling.
Nothing much is happening,
All I do is napping.

I'm always eating,
I'm cold, turn up the heating.
I am so skinny,
I can't afford a Mini.

I have no hobbies,
I'm afraid of bobbies.
I can't swim,
It's why I'm so dim.

I want to be a dentist,
I want to be a scientist,
I want to be an actor,
I want to be a doctor.

Deborah Clarke (12)
Burlish Middle School

HOMEWORK

Charlie left his homework,
At home today again;
The tenth time in succession,
And the teacher's gone insane!

Mary's been to Timbuktu,
She's left her homework there;
The teacher's going really mad,
She's pulling out her hair!

David says his dog's eaten it,
'I'll kill my little Rex';
The teacher makes a painful noise,
And snaps her dusty specs!

'I've done my homework,' Richard says,
'Come over here and see,'
The teacher takes a breath then faints,
She's off to casualty!

Josh Vale (12)
Burlish Middle School

MY CINQUAIN POEM

Predator
Lurking suspiciously
Gleaming orange coat
Pouncing for a meal
Fox.

Jamie Bevans (12)
Burlish Middle School

THE SOUND OF THE WIND

The sound of the wind is like a whistle,
Or a whoosh, a wish or a swish,
The wind tumbles by, stinging my eyes,
Blowing my hair out behind.

Walking down the road the wind tumbling by,
Making me wonder where it comes from,
Does it come from clouds or further up?
I wonder where it comes from.

The sound of the wind is like a dog's howl,
A splash of the sea or the hoot of an owl,
The wind makes me wonder,
The wind makes my mind drift,
I think the wind is a wonderful sound.

Victoria Rodwell (12)
Burlish Middle School

THE SEA

The sea comes rushing to the shore,
its beautiful colour dazzling in the sun.
The foamy waves splashing to and fro,
its icy temperature makes everything seem cold.
As the sun was setting in the sky,
the sea was coming closer and closer.
When finally the sea could come no more,
it began to retreat further and further away.
Until, at last, the sea comes rushing to the shore.

Natalie Bishop (12)
Burlish Middle School

THE SEA SPIRIT

As I looked out over the sea,
I saw the seagulls circling,
I heard the waves calling out to me,
Singing an eternal song,
The atmosphere was calm and tranquil,
A faint rumbling could be heard,
It grew stronger and louder,
Disturbing all the birds,
A giant mist arose from the water,
It danced around eerily,
It was followed closely by an earth-shattering scream,
It spoke to me in a thousand voices,
The voices of its prey,
The lost spirits beckoned me over,
I refused, then,
The sea spirit was lost forever.

Carla Valler-Jones (13)
Burlish Middle School

THE DIFFERENCES OF THE SEA

The sea is old as old can be,
It's seen many a battle in its life,
And it's never been friend or foe;
The sea is gigantic,
It is fierce and calm,
It can be helpful or can be hard,
It's cold, it's warm;
There are sharks and fish, small and large,

There could be war in the north,
Or peace in the south,
In the north there's a smell of death,
In the south there's a feeling of calm.
The sea is shallow and deep,
And green, red, black and blue;
But overall the sea is strange;
It's very very strange.

Rob Williams (12)
Burlish Middle School

THE HIP

I saw an old man standing on his ship,
This was the man with the missing hip,
Peering down into the deep, dark sea
Curious as can be.

Every day he was there, the same spot,
Fishing out boots and an old broken pot.
What was down there of much need?
Fishes, rusty things covered in seaweed.

One day he did not appear,
So I got out my snorkelling gear,
And paddled in the ocean blue
Amongst the rocks and the squelchy goo.

There I found it all alone,
The rotting remains of a bone.

Nikki Greenwood (13)
Burlish Middle School

AN EXPERIENCE

Moving swiftly through the water,
Never stopping, got to get further,
Mooring up at the end of the day,
Moving our own special way.

When we start moving once again,
Through wind, snow, sun or rain,
We'll have some wobbles and loads of bumps,
Steps and locks and also jumps.

It's hard to push the stiff old locks,
Don't get grounded on the rocks,
The key may be hard to push,
When winding it down, don't rush.

Stacey Green (12)
Burlish Middle School

THE SEA

The swiftly swerving curving sea,
with waves as slaves protecting all she owns.
The sea she moves with grace and style,
attracting people with her smile.
She makes them smile,
then in a while,
they get up, go for a swim,
hoping to wash away their sin.
The swiftly swerving curving sea,
with waves as slaves protecting all she owns.

Catherine Homer (12)
Burlish Middle School

THE RAGING SEA

The raging sea crashes against the cliffs
Beating an unsteady rhythm.
A boat is coming through the mist
Breaking through the gloom,
The waves are violent but yet steady
In a way placid and calm

The boat comes into harbour
Through the raging sea,
The waves settle down
Calm and placid again
Oh! What a graceful place to be.

Claire Charlwood (12)
Burlish Middle School

THE SEA

The sea is roaring,
Swimming around helplessly,
Is a tiny fish.
Along comes a huge wave,
Water washes up seaweed
            on the beach,
Amongst the mass of green
            lies the little fish.
Still, lifeless.

Helen Poulton (12)
Burlish Middle School

SPIDER

The spider hides under the chair,
waiting for the dark to close in.
His beady eyes dart around the room,
nothing, all is still, the time has come.

The spider runs out across the room,
a small piece of coal stands in its way.
Someone is coming, the spider stays still,
footsteps come and go.

The spider tries to get away
from the light which now shines.
Footsteps are near the spider,
one second, the spider is squashed.

Lucie Nelson (13)
Burlish Middle School

NIGHT-TIME

Night-time rolls in,
Daylight flows out.
Then the moon,
The cold unforgiving moon suffocates the sun.
The stars are shining bright in the night,
I watch this all from my bedroom as I slowly drift off to sleep.

Emma Mayo (12)
Burlish Middle School

BEING WELSH

My accent is so sweet,
My language is so well-known,
It is such a treat,
Welsh cakes are thrown.

In spring the daffodils bloom,
In autumn the leaves fall.
In winter it's gloom,
But in summer don't forget your beach-ball.

So many hills, so many sheep,
At night the sky is full of colours.
In summer the horns wildly blow,
On the plain wild flowers bloom.

If I could fly with the seagulls,
I could see the world below me.
Sheep are Welsh, but not bulls,
In Wales I feel free.

As the waves touch the sky,
While I walk along my lonely way,
As the waves disappear, I wave *goodbye*,
Along the shores of Swansea Bay.

The sand is so gold,
The water is so cool.
Ice-cream goes mouldy,
Don't forget your beach tool.

Alison Higgins (15)
Christopher Whitehead High School

DAY BY NIGHT

Flying through the sky above,
Beauty held within that dove.
Windows glimmer within my view,
Grass glistening with humid dew.
Squirrels run from tree to tree,
Is it possible could it be?

My ears are blocked with endless noise,
Different races, girls and boys.
By noon the grass is green and dry,
Where is that dove, where does it fly?

As the breezy cold wind blows,
Could the weather change, who knows.
But then stars form and reach my sight.
As the day turns into night.

Jodie Marie Rice (16)
Christopher Whitehead High School

MAN UNITED

Man United are the best,
And they beat all the rest.
Newcastle they really struggle against.

Unmistakably in their red they
Never drop their heads.
I love them to the end.
The end I think will never come,
Even though they lose some.
Devils they are just like *me!*
In this world of football teams.

Thomas Siviter (13)
Comberton Middle School

THE WOOZLE

Among the plants and the trees,
The birds and the bees,
In the cave he called home,
Sat the woozle, all alone.

He sat in his cave, night and day,
Animals that went by, would be his prey,
He'd gobble them up, fat or lean,
Munching, crunching, he's very mean.

One day the woozle came from his cave,
Went to the river and found a slave,
He took it home and gobbled it up,
Unfortunately it came back up.

Never again he left his cave,
In case there was another slave,
So he went into a winter sleep,
Nothing could wake him it was so deep.

Alas one day the hunters came,
They wanted to train him, make him tame,
Off to a zoo the woozle went,
Into a cage the creature was sent.

The woozle lived his short life here,
People to him looked very queer,
He couldn't move, just had to peer,
And finished his short life just here.

Peter Mason (11)
Comberton Middle School

THE WORLD

The world is enormously huge,
It is mostly sea,
But why is it all named differently?
Why do people speak strange languages
And live in different places?
I don't know, do you?

If the world is a globe,
Why don't I fall off?
Why is North, North not South?
If the world is spinning,
Why don't I get dizzy?
I don't know, do you?

Why are all the islands and countries separate . . .?
Why aren't they all joined as one?
Why do people need to eat and drink?
Why do people bother?
All these questions about the earth and I can't
answer a single one,
Can you?

Clare Millard (11)
Comberton Middle School

EXAMS

Five minutes to go,
Until I have to take the test
I know my marks will be lower than the rest.

Tick-tock,
Just hear the clock.
My mind's in a whirr,
The words are a blur.

Tick-tock,
Again goes the clock,
Will I get an *A*, I just don't know,
But whatever I get I know it'll be low.

Ding-dong there goes the bell,
I'm sure that I did reasonably well
I was anxious I'm not anymore,
The reason is I got all ninety-four!

Adam Chester (12)
Comberton Middle School

THE OCEAN

Running down the beach,
Across the golden sand,
Feet burning like flames,
Leaping into a sparkling sea.

Wildly howling boys,
Splashing, thrashing, arms and legs,
Ducking and screaming,
Yelling and pleading.

A swift sharp dive,
From a lonely beach,
Through the centre of a furling wave,
Like a dolphin gliding along.

A surfer launches himself,
Sailing on a crest of foam,
Riding on the white horses,
The sparkling creatures carry him home.

Lowri Garratt (11)
Comberton Middle School

SHADOWS

Shadows in the kitchen,
Shadows on the stair,
Shadows in my bedroom,
Shadows everywhere.

Shadows can be comforting,
When I'm feeling down,
Shadows make me angry,
And make me want to frown.

Mine seems to be attached to me,
And what I think is queer,
Is it's there when the sun is out,
And when it's dark it will disappear.

It follows me wherever I go,
And never goes away,
It does whatever I'm doing,
And mouths whatever I say.

Shadows can look like different things,
Like a witch or even a crocodile,
But when they look like things like these,
I just break out in a smile!

Sarah McKeown (13)
Comberton Middle School

HOMETIME

Outside the rain is pouring down
But in this classroom we are all snug and dry.
Suddenly the bell goes
We all dash to the door
Leaving teacher flat on the floor.

We rush to our pegs
Then run down the path
We leap on the bus
For we are all in a rush.
The engine starts up
We wave to our friends
For school time today has come to an end.

John Pochribniak (11)
Comberton Middle School

WORLDWIDE DESTRUCTION

Day by day people hunt,
Making the world a piece of junk,
Killing elephants for their tusks,
Burning forests as the animals run,
Some don't escape whining for help,
As the flames eat the forest away.

Day by day some things becoming extinct,
Tigers, rhinos, elephants, great African bears,
People kill and hunt, the animals will
Never see light again,
People like us, are slowly killing our world.

Day by day greedy fishermen,
Cast their nets,
They don't care about fish,
They just kill to have on their dish,
Lots of fish.
It's us who will wipe out the seaworld
If we're not careful.

Paul Brookes (11)
Comberton Middle School

WHO ARE YOU?

When I see another person,
I wonder who they are.
Are they human?
Are they robots?
Are they there at all?

Am I the only human?
Did the rest die out?
Am I on another planet,
Transported late at night?

Perhaps everyone's a hologram,
There to see how I react.
Maybe everyone's an alien,
In a clever disguise.

Sometimes I wonder,
Could all this be true?
Maybe everyone is human,
Maybe it's me who's not . . .

Paul Lovell (12)
Comberton Middle School

THE CHASE OF THE LION

The lion stalks its prey.
The deer runs away into the bushes.
The lion chases it away.

The deer is still and
the lion goes in for the kill.
At last! He captures it.

The lion's pinned him down
with one blow from his mighty paw.
The deer is now dead.

Susan Baker (11)
Comberton Middle School

THE WHALE

Mid-Atlantic, way out at sea,
A sperm whale drifts quite close to me.
I'm a deep sea diver, so you see . . .
A sperm whale drifts quite close to me.

The sperm whale swims around with kin
As it brushes past my shin.
Suddenly, danger lurks behind,
Quick - dash - swim and hide.

A monster squid comes from the deep
And lets out an ear-piercing, high-pitched shriek.
A cloud of black comes from the squid
And covers me. Oh yes, it did!

The squid starts diving straight at me.
The sperm whale rockets past me.
The whale opens its jaws and takes a bite,
The squid dives away and gives up the fight.

I swim way back to my boat,
Come up to the surface and there I float.
Mid-Atlantic, way out at sea,
A sperm whale drifts quite close to me.

Nicholas J Crumpton (11)
Comberton Middle School

THE FOUR SEASONS

In the sunny, autumn sky where
White clouds move across swiftly,
Winds blow gently through trees
With colour changing leaves.
Green to orange and there is red
And brown they fall to be widespread.

Seasons change and winter is here,
It is cold and sometimes severe.
Skies go grey and the sun despairs,
It will take some time doing repairs.
Animals hide inside bare trees,
As land and water is in a freeze.

Winter is conquered thanks to spring
Which is now a seasonal king.
Animals and nature revives
Which they can easily survive.
March, April, May are the months,
Which they appear in a year, once.

Seasons have a new ruler,
Now summer takes over.
The summer casts a warm spell,
The animals cannot repel.
All persons go to the cool beach,
That is the best place they could reach.

Thomas Lai (11)
Comberton Middle School

THE LIVING OF THE DEAD

Where souls and spirits come to rest,
Trick or Treaters in fancy dress.
In gloomy tombs and shallow graves,
And spirits in their dark, dark caves.

The witching hour is close at hand,
And the hourglass runs out of sand.
The witches swoop, sail and glide,
And on the land they run to hide.

Ghosts and phantoms glide back to tombs,
Back to the dark mist and gloom.
The relatives of the dead go back to mourn,
As the night, of course, turns to dawn.

Gemma Smith (11)
Comberton Middle School

THE OWL

It hides itself away by day
And comes out at night,
It has soft wings to muffle
The sound of the flight.

In the night it swoops down low
Its claws ready to hunt,
It sees a mouse down below
It zooms down and catches it.

With its claws wrapped tightly around the mouse
The mouse begins to suffer,
The owl is content
And his catch is now his supper.

Louise Howes (12)
Comberton Middle School

FOOD

Have you ever had warm ice-cream
or cold tomato soup?
Rotten lettuce or smelly cheese
runny mashed potato or solid stew?

Spaghetti and meatballs, mouldy bananas,
lumpy custard, brussel sprouts?
Snail sauce, frog's leg trifle,
jam and chicken on toast?

Gravy with yoghurt, tomato sauce with cereal,
oranges garnished with beetroot and beans?
Lemon juice with chocolate and squid,
and of course egg and pickle sandwiches?

Hayley Slater (11)
Comberton Middle School

SKIING

As the chair-lift goes up the mountain,
I watch the people skiing down.
One person goes tumbling over,
And another ten fall too.

As the lift goes round the bend,
I quickly hop off and get ready to ski
And go to the top of the hill,
I push myself and off I go.

The wind brushed back my cheeks,
As I shot down the mountain top speed.
In a flash I was at the bottom,
Ready to go again.

Emily Markham (11)
Comberton Middle School

KITTENS

Look at your little tail,
Look at your little paws,
Look at your little ears,
And look at your little claws.
Look at your little head,
And look at your little nose,
And look at your tiny, little toes.

Look at you playing on the bin,
Playing with a silver tin.
Hitting, scratching,
The tin falls off,
Then you let out a little cough.

Look at you running across the garden,
Full of glee.
It looks like you're smiling straight at me,
I laugh,
You fall over,
And eat a piece of clover.

Kittens are so funny,
And so cute,
They're playful and happy,
And usually minute.

David Koker (11)
Comberton Middle School

THE HEDGEHOG

It comes out at night,
When the sky is very dark.
It scurries around quietly,
And the dog starts to bark.

It has a thousand prickles,
Upon its dark brown back.
It rolls into a ball when it is scared,
And thinks it will be attacked.

In autumn it hibernates,
And all through the winter months.
It curls up into a ball of leaves,
And falls asleep almost at once.

I love the hedgehog that comes into my garden,
And has a snuffle around.
If I had some money for every time it came,
I would have a million pounds!

Laura Thomas (11)
Comberton Middle School

PARENTS

Parents are crazy
all they do is nag
you never know what's coming next
nag, nag, nag!

'Go and do your homework!'
'Tidy your room now'
This life is so boring
nag, nag, nag!

Do they like nagging?
Don't they get bored?
Do parents find it most amusing to
nag, nag, nag!

Parents should be pleasant
and should respect their children more
nag, nag, nag!

Katie Andrews (11)
Comberton Middle School

SPACE

Zooming through space
a billion miles an hour.
Lots of little shining stars
Rushing by the window.

Oh dear asteroid belt!
Left! Left! Right! Left! Left! Right!
Manage to get through
without trouble.

I can see lots of little
flying saucers
Little green aliens waving at me
while I wave back.

Finally landing on the Earth
coming down to the ground.
Good to see all the people,
feet on terra firma.

David Lane (11)
Comberton Middle School

OUT ON THE PLAYGROUND

Out on the playground,
Eating my tuck,
Down came a seagull,
And I ran out of luck.

Out on the playground,
There's a dog running loose,
Watch out Barry,
He's after your mousse!

Out on the playground,
Watching the brawl,
'I think he'll win'
'Naa! He won't win at all.'

Out on the playground,
Running around,
Teacher won't catch me,
Oh no, I've slipped to the ground!

Whistle's gone,
Everybody line up!

Richard Anderson (13)
Comberton Middle School

THE PIG SLIMMER

As a pig I know
people call me a slob.
I have swill three times a day,
I must look like a blob.

I decided to eat low fat swill,
I took little bites.
The farmer thought that I was mad,
The first pig to go on a diet.

A week has gone by,
I am half as fat.
There is a beauty show in town,
I will enter that.

I get up on the stage,
I hear quite a lot of sniggers but,
I am the world's slimmest pig.
I turn out the winner.

Catriona Malcolm (11)
Comberton Middle School

HOMEWORK MACHINE

Homework comes round every night,
Some of it gives me such a fright,
Some teachers are cruel and some are mean,
They think of me as a homework machine.

I start it early and finish it late,
My parents get in such a state,
They want me to go to bed and rest,
But I can't because I have to revise for a test.

I get up in the morning still feeling shattered,
But I have done my homework, and to the teachers,
        that's all that mattered,
They look fresh and ready for the day,
But I am not, I must say.

Friday night comes, hip hip hooray,
I can leave my homework until another day,
But please will you let me say,
I will now have to rest and play.

Gemma Davies (12)
Comberton Middle School

SAVE THE ANIMALS

The bear, the tiger, the mouse and rat,
The lion, the monkey, the dog and cat,
They all will start to fade away,
And perhaps they will all be gone one day.

All the animals of the sea,
Will die as well unless they flee,
Think of the whale and the shark,
Soon their world will go all dark.

The thrush, the robin and the lark,
All start to pass out over Sark,
If a tree falls a bird loses its home,
Leaving it with nothing, all left alone.

Come on we've got to stop this now,
All the farm animals, even the cow!
It had to happen the world has toppled down,
Now the King of the Jungle has lost his crown.

Tim Willetts (11)
Comberton Middle School

VESUVIOUS ERUPTS

The mountain erupts from far down inside,
The people of Pompeii, try to run and hide,
Why is this monster attacking their town?
What is it that's slithering and hunting them down?

The earth is shaking underneath their feet,
Their world is exploding, they know they are beat,
Within seconds they will be swallowed whole,
By this strange, mean creature, burning their soles.

They scream and they cry, they run and they yell,
But what is this liquid, coming from Hell?
Can nobody help them, can no one survive?
I think not, they are buried alive.

Adele Cro (13)
Comberton Middle School

FOODS

All the foods I like to eat,
I like the veg,
I like the meat
Some hot, some cold,
Some new, some old.
Snacks and sweets
Pies and flans
And helping hands
To cook the meals
And jellied eels,
Bangers and mash
Are rather flash
Chicken wings
Are fit for kings.
The food on my plate
Is rather great,
Breakfast and lunch,
Dinner and brunch,
At any time I will eat
Any food,
Any veg,
Anything!

Andrew Ireland (12)
Comberton Middle School

ALIENS!

Aliens live in outer-space,
Coming down in UFOs,
Shining lights on chosen people,
Taking them into their spaceships.

Where do aliens come from?
Is it from the future?
Do they come from outer-space?
Are they small and green?

How fast can aliens travel?
Is it the speed of light?
As we explore the moon,
Does that make us aliens?

Zooming through the universe,
Coming down to planets,
Trying to invade,
But not always succeeding.

Matthew Vaughan (11)
Comberton Middle School

AUTUMN

The autumn leaves are changing,
From green to yellow and gold,
They spread out like an ocean,
With colours true and bold.

The grass looks clear and fresh,
In the misty morning light,
With cobwebs dancing merrily,
Oh what a beautiful sight.

The clouds are high up in the sky,
It looks like rain today,
It's not very bright in fact it's dull,
In a gloomy sort of way.

The setting sun's a picture,
Or so I have been told,
With a multitude of colours,
Red and crimson, emerald and gold.

Gemma Cannock (12)
Comberton Middle School

DREAMS

I once had a dream,
I was a beautiful queen,
I once had a dream,
I was swimming in ice-cream,
I once had a dream,
I was kissed by a sunbeam,
I once had a dream,
I was hit by a wooden beam,
I once had a dream,
I was in a dream,
I once had a dream,
And it was all about cream,
I once had a dream,
And it was all about *you!*

Charlotte Waldron (12)
Comberton Middle School

PARENTS

Were they crazy,
Strange or cool,
Sad or daggy,
What were they like?

All they
tell us is
'You're too young.'
But 'cos they never tell
I ask Gran!

Acting weirdly,
Late nights out?
Pictures of them with long hair
and flowers in the background. Mmm?

When I find Dad's diary
I read, bizarre light,
zany music and
way-out fashions!

In the wardrobe I find
flares, hot-pants, platforms?
Now I know what they were,
They were *hippies!*

Jonathan Buckerfield (12)
Comberton Middle School

THE WALK TO SCHOOL

The door shuts behind me,
The street looks long and narrow,
I look up at the huge oak tree,
I am positive it is staring at me.

The stone which I kick down the street bounces along,
It's lifeless, it's tiresome,
I wish it could change into a football,
At Wembley, with the flashing floodlights.

I can now see the gates,
The whiteness is petrifying,
The slabs are broken and cracked,
The bush alongside the path is dead.

The crowds are now gathering,
They start to shout,
They are going into the playground now,
The long trip is over for them.

The school bell rings,
I run for the doors,
I imagine it's the one hundred metres,
The doors are the line.

I almost make it,
But then I fall over,
The perfect steps in front of me,
Another day of torture begins.

David Cadwallader (11)
Comberton Middle School

THE WEATHER

Look at the sky, how blue is it?
Look at the birds that chirp in it.
Look at the clouds that darken it.
How bright is the sun in the sky today?

Look at the clouds, how dark are they?
Is there rain falling there today?
Is it dim or very dark?
Not fog, I hope blocking our way.

The weather changes day by day.
We can try and predict it but can't be sure.
The world would be lost without the weather.
We sometimes dither but we love the weather.

Sam Beasley (11)
Comberton Middle School

WHY IS IT?

Why is it that the sky is blue?
Why is no one the same as you?
Why is there so much famine and war?
Why are there so many sick and poor?
Why is it that we are here now?
Why is it that we can always say how?
Why is it we have three meals a day?
Why is it so, I cannot say . . .
Why is it that we drive here and there?
Why is it, we pollute the air?
Why am I making such a fuss?
The simple answer is *because* . . .

Thomas Brown (12)
Comberton Middle School

OH, WHAT CAN IT BE?

It stands there in the corner,
Looking straight at me,
It flashes different colours,
Oh, what can it be?

It has a switch to start the lights,
Set the colours free,
It has a weird control pad,
Oh, what can it be?

I can see brilliant images,
Jumping out at me,
Very weird noises,
Oh, what can it be?

It makes me laugh and makes me cry,
It makes me want to be
In all the action,
Oh, what can it be?

It stands there in the corner,
Looking straight at me,
It flashes different colours,
It's my very own TV!

Sarah Handley (12)
Comberton Middle School

IT'S ALL OUTSIDE

It's raining
Outside
The sun is shining
Outside
Spring is coming
Outside
A bird is singing
Outside
The moon is shining in the dark
Outside
Raindrops running down the window
Outside
Trees rustling in the wind
Outside
Bright stars at night
Outside
Snow is falling
Outside
The bells are ringing
Outside
People sing
Outside
But I am inside.

Naomi Jarman (12)
Comberton Middle School

30 MINUTES LEFT TO LIVE

Twelve years I've lived my life,
I haven't even found a wife!
I was intending to buy a car,
But if I'm dead I won't get far.
Half an hour that's not long,
When I'm dead I'll sing no song!

I was also planning to get a job,
And so I'd earn a couple of bob.
I might have ended up digging up coal,
Well at least I won't be on the Dole.
But I might have been very rich,
Isn't life such a bitch!

I might have had kids if I was lucky,
Playing in the mud getting very mucky.
I could give them pocket money,
And make them believe in the Easter Bunny.
At Christmas time we'd have such fun,
I would get drunk on sherry and rum!

Ten minutes now the clock is ticking,
I don't care I'm alive and kicking.
But I'll look on the bright side,
Five minutes with nowhere to hide.
Time's up, I'm six foot under,
What would happen to me . . . I wonder.

Mark Jones (12)
Comberton Middle School

SCHOOL

Why bother to go to school?
It hasn't even got a pool.
You have to learn maths and all,
And even go to the assembly hall.

Everyone waits until she says,
You go outside, so everyone plays.
At the end of break she blows the whistle,
For everyone to stand still and then dismissal.

In lesson time we write and learn,
I hear everyone's head tick and churn.
In maths we always get a test,
There's no time to have a rest.

At half-past three there's endless flows,
Of children everywhere and then it goes.
After school there's lots of sports,
Even squash and tennis courts.

Is there a reason why we go to school,
Even though there is no pool?
Yes of course there is, to learn,
And make our heads tick and churn!

Louise Allchurch (13)
Comberton Middle School

FOOTBALL

People go crazy,
People go wild,
When a goal is scored.

Some people just get bored.
Teams are happy,
Teams are sad.

Players get paid lots of money,
This case is not funny,
Football clubs get lots too.

Kicking a ball on a field,
Goals are scored sometimes not,
Every goal means a lot.

If you play football for money,
Or for fun,
The pressure involved is like a tonne.

Chris MacDonald (12)
Comberton Middle School

THE FIRE

A fire alarm screaming loud,
A smoky smell is all around,
A dangerous feeling in the air,
Walking around taking great care.

The sirens coming up the road,
How it started no one knows,
My sister yelling from next door,
A roaring from under the floor.

A man in red starts to call,
I ventured out into the hall,
Lifted up by big gentle arms,
Thank goodness for my smoke alarm.

Stood there watching my house burn away,
No hope of seeing it the next day,
I sat in hospital safe at last,
Thinking what has just gone past.

Gemma Parker (13)
Comberton Middle School

CAMOUFLAGED SNAKE

Camouflaged snake lying in the sun,
Animals can't see him so they don't run.
His tongue jumps out and goes back in,
The animal gets closer and the snake pounces.
The snake injects venom and the animal's dead,
It opens its mouth and the animal disappears.
There's a lump in the snake's body and it starts to digest.
The lump disappears and the snake slithers off,
And disappears into the distance.

James Brookes (12)
Fairfield High School

DARKNESS FALLS ON LONDON, WINTER

As I slip out into the cold and evil night,
Rubbish and leaves dance escorted by the wind.
I passed an old tramp, a sad expression possessed his face.
A frozen tear lingered in his eye, ready to fall to the stone-cold ground.
The cold winter was biting my skin.
It felt like my blood had frozen and then shattered.
It was certain that winter had grasped London.
Fog - winter's cold breath lingered over the dismal city.
The silver moon smiled down on the world.
Although it looked cold and lonely sharing its empire with the stars,
The stars twinkled like a million lost-and-found souls,
Found by the gentle shepherd God.

Amy Wheeler (12)
Fairfield High School

IN THAT WORLD

In that world,
There is a jungle full of noises,
Birds of paradise call,
Amazing flowers galore,
Blossoming trees grow tall,
Then a chainsaw begins to roar.
Silence reigns.
Then a tree completes its fall,
Some rare animals are no more.
This is our world,
Soon there will be no trees to fall,
Then part of our world will be no more.

Joanne Edwards (12)
Fairfield High School

THE UNKNOWN - WHAT WOULD HAVE BEEN

Happy and excited for a
little life growing unknown
to the world except those
who are close to you.

Planning for the change, making
room and space, a smile on
everyone's face.

Going to a place all white
inside, with a distinctive smell
that you kind of remember.
You come to a room full of sadness and hurt.
Seeing those eyes with water flowing like a river from them,
with those eyes comes a face,
a face of the unknown.

Tavline McDonough (15)
Fairfield High School

THE OLD OAK TREE

The sun shines down on the old oak tree
It's been there much longer than you or me.
In the summer it gives shade for sheep and cows
And a home for birds within its boughs.

In autumn the leaves start to fall,
But still it stands there broad and tall.
The sheep and cows have now all gone
And birds have flown with their song.

In the winter, as far as I know
It does not do anything, not even grow.
It still stands there through day and night
And is first to catch the morning light.

In spring at first it looks bare and lean
But soon there appears new buds of green.
Standing as seasons come and go
Through summer sunshine and winter snow.

Rachel Price-Greenow (14)
Fairfield High School

DESPISED IMAGERY

Hay-making in the afternoon sun, laughing, playing,
Having fun with the old bat and ball, laughing, playing,
Planting potatoes in the barren soil, laughing, playing.
Oh how I admired him so.

Playing a game of cards, a simple trick,
Lighting the coal fire.
Cooking liver - how I hated liver,
Oh how I loved him so.

Now, the house is empty.
The hay is gone to waste.
The garden choked with weeds.
The card game is finished.
The fire; put out.

Christopher Jenkins (15)
Fairfield High School

SATURDAY AFTERNOON

Wicket, brown and alone,
A sea of green,
Doors, open,
      Changing room
Deserted.
In silence, change street clothes for 'whites'.
Studded boots clattering tiled floor,
Filling with team-mates' banter.
          Captain,
'We're batting
Open
Plenty of time
Look at it.'

Put on pads,
Box and gloves,
Pick up bat,
And out.

Take guard,
The field is silent.

Tom Ward (15)
Fairfield High School

SUNSET

A long straight black line of a horizon,
A deep red sun - only a sliver,
Colours merging together,
Streaks of cloud dyed red and purple,
A horse rears up to meet the coloured sky.

Gemma A Weeks (12)
Fairfield High School

WHY HER?

I think about it wondering why I feel this way,
Every day there's something new to think about
Maybe it's just me or someone else,
Never knowing of what love I have
It would stay and never escape.
To see it like a vision in a dream
Not showing what I see
Like my heart has been ripped at the seam,
I never knew and in a way it hurts to live without her.
But life goes on and the memories
I wish I had, too hard to erase,
Knowing past life, is sometimes
something to smile about,
To remember,
Not knowing why my question will
never be answered.

Natalie Mark (15)
Fairfield High School

THE CLOCK

The clock hangs on the wall,
Tick tock, tick tock
In a silent kitchen quiet and still,
Tick tock, tick tock.
It sits there for hours and hours on end,
Until the children come home from school.
You can't hear the tick tock, tick tock
Of the ticking clock anymore.

Rebecca Jones (12)
Fairfield High School

CHEETAH

I could see where his sweat had matted his fur to his warm flesh.
The morning light glinted off his grey-brown cloak.
And in one graceful movement all my energy pulsed into my legs.
I focused upon his ugly head;
And I hated him;
Hated him for his imperfection;
Hated him for his gross posture;
And most of all I hated him for being an animal as I was.
My limbs beat upon the dry ground, as my elegant body arched
                                                    through the air.
The dumb animals scattered in every direction.
My personal one veered left, his bulky body falling in place
                                    behind his terror-stricken eyes.
All my sense of direction was gone, the only thought in my mind
                                    was to kill this beast for his sins.
I leapt and my claws bit deep into his throat - and he howled:
Such was his howl that for a split second I questioned my actions . . .
Then I bit deeper,
Silence;
And he flopped to the floor making a final frantic kick on impulse.

Llewelyn Watkins (12)
Fairfield High School

THE BEGINNING

An eternity,
Motionless and silent.
Waiting . . .
It's trivial hollow continuance.
An existence of solitude.
Time; what time; no time.
The boundless abyss.

A vast explosion,
The vast explosion!
The fuse of humanity,
The source of time.
And sent forth from the cauldron of fire,
Was life!

Paul Archer (12)
Fairfield High School

SILENT LISTENER

Drifting on the tranquil water
mothered like a newborn
Pleasant sun drowning this land
Lazy water drags its feet in the afternoon sun
The cosy harbour's pastel buildings
shine like precious jewels
Glistening and shimmering
all still, hot and forgotten
Worries melt away into carefree waters
Forever my silent listener
lost in time and thought
The palms drowsily nod in my honour
safe from the mighty sea and wind
protected from harm
looked over by a forever smiling light
waiting to take my hand
to guide me home
in the midst of this tranquillity
I turn, I leave my silent listener;
The land sleeps on.

Kerry Havard (15)
Fairfield High School

UNDER THE SURFACE OF THE SEA

Under the surface of the sea,
Lies a whole new world for me.
There are whales and dolphins everywhere,
Little fish darting here and there.
The crabs walk sideways across the sand,
Their bodies larger than my hand.
There are mysteries way down deep,
Strange fish with secrets they will keep.
The seaweed dances side to side,
Brightly coloured coral gives places to hide.
The mussels cling to the rocks in clumps,
While limpets cover them with their humps.
Under the surface of the sea,
Night or day whatever it be,
What an interesting place this is for me.

Aimee Watson (12)
Fairfield High School

THAT SPOILT PATH

Walking along the open path
looking across the moorlands,
not a sound to be heard.

Only one thing that spoils the path,
the sight of u-shaped prints,
hundreds of them - scattered as far as I can see.

Then I glance away from it,
to see a herd.
Dust flew in a cloud, the birds flew,
then, all there was, one hundred scattered prints,
a galloping herd of wild ponies.

Carolyn Jellard (14)
Fairfield High School

SAILING THROUGH AIR

On a sunny day,
On an airfield,
Small white clouds accumulate.

Birds soaring,
Engines roaring,
The flight-tower's calling.

We strap ourselves in,
We're about to begin,
The tug-plane starts its engine.

We taxi out,
Straighten up,
And wait for the tug to roar.

A sudden jolt,
The rope tightens,
At forty knots we're up.

Alongside flies a buzzard,
Spinning, spinning, round and round,
Like a Catherine wheel on the fifth.

A sudden sink,
It's time to land,
Glide path steepens, I see the ground.

Air speed bleeds like a dying man,
Then like death, we stop,
The wing falls down,
The flight is over.

James Ewins (15)
Fairfield High School

THE UNIVERSE

Unimaginably vast
Nothingness stretching for eternity
Teeming with the swirling bodies of planets,
Stars and asteroids
Airless and unexplored.

Its birth unknown
Its end unthinkable
Literally eternal
Dotted with the hidden terrors of black holes,
Bending space and time
Completely alien to our minds.

Are we alone
Or are we neighbours to races
Superior or inferior to our own;
And are they too thinking;
Is there anyone out there?

Caleb Jones (13)
Fairfield High School

PEOPLE

There are some things,
that I could say
about the way people act
and the way people play.

Occasionally I think,
everyone's the same,
two feet, two hands,
but a different name.

Then I think
how can this be true,
we all are different,
including you.

Sarah Burt (15)
Fairfield High School

I USED TO LIVE HERE ONCE

Tall, splendour palm trees,
Sway in the gentle sea breeze,
Exquisite colourful flowers,
Indigo, purple passion, turquoise,
Blending in with the sun's rays.

Sun-bleached sands,
Crystal clear water,
Glistening and shimmering,
In the sun,
Untouched by man.

Sweet scent of flowers,
Coconuts, sun cream,
Combining into one exotic
Tropical fragrance,
Meandering around the stone-washed buildings.

Bumpy, dusty dirt tracks,
With horse and carts
Being driven over,
Disturbing and unsettling
The dust.

Emma Bowell (14)
Fairfield High School

THROUGH THE DOOR

I've never been behind that door,
I wonder what there is,
It is such a mystery,
A fantasy world or reality?
I'll open it and see,
Turn the handle, open it up,
I see a wall of ocean,
I step inside and am suddenly swimming
Within the unknown depths,
Fish are all around me,
Thinking as I wonder 'What's at the end of this?'
It's peaceful down here,
I feel comfortable,
No one of my kind,
If I stay here long enough who knows what I might find?
The water is getting thinner,
I think the journey is over,
I see the door in front of me,
This is the end of my adventure.

Gemma Powell (14)
Fairfield High School

THE DEEP BLUE SEA

I love to go down diving
To look at the life that's below
Down around the greenest seaweed
What I will see I never can tell.

Down among the fish I swim
In their natural habitat they be.
I love to be with them swimming
Down in the deep blue sea.

I wish I were a fish myself,
But that will never be true.
I pray every night I become one,
But I am surely wasting my time.

Lee Owen (14)
Fairfield High School

YOUR HANDS

Your hands are thick and large,
Working hands,
Worn after years of building,
Not white, not really red,
But pink and wrinkly,
With lots of cuts and bruises,
From working all day and night.

I watch you working,
Making windows, doors and chairs,
Your hands work so quick and steady,
Never going wrong,
Always doing the right thing.

Your hands are very strong,
But also very calm,
When I see them,
I see reliable hands,
Which never let you down
When you need them.

Alice Lewis (14)
Fairfield High School

THE RAILWAY

Early morning sunrise
Coldness in the air
No people on the platform
The train does not stop there.

Flying through the countryside
Without a worry or care
On rails like a silver snake
Cross them if you dare!

A tunnel coming close
The engine whistles here
And then it's dark and damp
Before she's in the clear.

My train will go forever,
Until I turn it off,
'If only you were real' I think
As I hold my engine aloft.

Chris Oakley (14)
Fairfield High School

POEM

There I sat in an empty space
watching my life slip away.
Nothing to be done, all I could do was just sit
there and watch.
Mistakes that were made and covered up.
Mistakes that were made but nothing could be
done to change them or me.
Old faces and new faces coming and going from my life.
Each day goes by, I'll take it step by step.

Ian Davies (15)
Fairfield High School

HANG GLIDING

Fly like an eagle,
swoop like a bird,
upping and downing,
like music unheard.

With almost a freedom,
almost unchained,
only stopped by the wind,
that's never the same.

Alone, on your own,
and with you no care,
with your thoughts for company,
as if you weren't there.

The bearer the wind,
the choirboys the birds,
the sky is the roof of the
church of the world.

The ground homes in to view,
you dock with a jar,
the sails are furled up,
and tied to the spar.

The end of the voyage,
the end of the flight,
back to the chains,
and the problems of life.

Michael Watkins (14)
Fairfield High School

THE SEA

Light filtered down,
Through the water,
Shells were broken,
With opened oysters,
Near the frilly pearl oysters.

The bitter wind,
With the rippling sea,
The bed which filled,
With such riches,
The cured wars,
Decorated churches.

For the power,
For the poor,
Of this world today,
For our sakes,
And for our souls.

Gemma Heighway (14)
Fairfield High School

PURE MAGIC

I see a door, brown tacky, unvarnished looking door.
Through that door
A room I saw just a large room pale and bare,
The windows misted white and pure,
I could not look as the scenes were obscure.

Through that door I wished to see a coal fire
Blazing, and glittering trees, no muttering, no sound, just complete
Silence.

This was strange, it was like heaven was right in my door,
Through that door, I could see a city of mine,
The place I was born, the place I grew up.

Through that door was me, once more,
Wondering whether my pure magic could come alive
Once more.

Victoria Robinson (14)
Fairfield High School

I LIVED HERE ONCE

There in amazement
a lot had differed,
huge wooden house,
white pillars,
holding it all up.

A big green lawn
in front of me
golden leaves
showering the green blades.
Breeze floating past
clear blue sky matching it all.

Familiar laughs
come back to me
happy, sad memories
an overwhelming feeling comes.
I lived here once.

Zoe Smith (15)
Fairfield High School

THE LADY ON THE MOOR

The choking mist began to clear,
The waters stilled, and somewhere near
A chill wind struck the blackened moor -
Just like so many times before.
The man began to feel the chill,
Drew close his coat, as from the hill
A ghostly figure descends . . .

> The man recalled the silhouette
> From distant, younger days, but yet
> The girl was young, and old was he:
> 'This recognition cannot be!'
> He pulled upon his woollen tie,
> And as he blinked both bright blue eyes
> The girl averts her gaze . . .

She looked at him, with pleading stare,
The breeze blew through her raven hair,
And as she turned to face the lake,
The man perceived, 'twas no mistake,
He'd definitely seen before
The solemn maid upon the moor -
The figure by the lake . . .

> She walked up to the murky lake,
> The man's whole frame began to shake,
> She held her hands aloft her head -
> And in an instant her vision was dead.
> The old man saw her, and there she stays,
> She haunts the shoreline to this day . . .
> *The Lady on the Moor.*

Bethan Jones (14)
Fairfield High School

PREDATOR

Head tilted to one side,
Still,
Soft, long fur moves in the rustling breeze.
Eyes like a hawk
Set on an object.

Hackles on high,
Ready to pounce,
Ears as sharp, as needles,
Able to hear the softest sound.

Claws, gripping the earth
Below,
As sharp as talons,
Ready to kill.

Gareth Mussell (14)
Fairfield High School

WHEN I AM OLD

I want to sing Oasis songs
When walking down Church Street.
And wink at men and clap my hands
And laugh at those I meet.
I want to take off all my clothes
And dance in Merry Hill
Wear just a smile in Body Shop
As I wait to pay my bill.
But my chance to shock will have to wait
While parents still harshly scold.
My granny strips off all the time
So will I when I am old.

Laura Hartwell (17)
Haybridge High School

DREAMS

In years to come I'll sit and watch
the wind blow through the trees.
I'll relax have fun,
not think or run,
and take pleasure in squashing bees.

Stand up to the man from next door,
his muttering and tuttering I'll add,
'Hey sir, after all it's not such a chore!'
To stop him from going mad.

I'll wait in the traffic,
not hooting or tooting and smile at the
passers-by.
Chew on my nails, not care what I'm doing
and idly gaze at the sky.

But can we live in a world of no stress
not worry or care about dress?
If we learnt ways not to be led,
a lot more could be said.

Emma Williams (18)
Haybridge High School

SATIN COATED CLOWN

Railroad trolley, bobbing up and down,
Old ladies' stockings, wrinkled knees falling down.
Bright red lipstick, deep satin coat,
Hysterical laugh as he charges about.
A peck and a peek, a bobbety run.
Face like a clown, a symbol of fun.

Victoria Stack (17)
Haybridge High School

HYLAS AND THE NYMPHS

Long groomed hair,
Clear as crystal the water.
Ruby lips contrast the ghostly white skin, always, always.

Sun filters through dark green canopies,
Ripples rise, surfacing,
Forever travelling to the ends of time.

Belt of red,
Silky smooth, ripples of silk red upon cloth,
Sounds of flesh against flesh,
Gentle creatures of the river,
Playing playfully.

I see sadness,
Yet love for one,
A playful splash,
A sad little smile.
Ruby lips contrast the ghostly white skin, always, always.

Sickly sweet, the smell of lilies,
In the trees a frog leaps another.
Life is blossoming,
But love of one is dying,
Belt of red the symbol.

The water will always be there.

Meredyth Boxwell (17)
Haybridge High School

POEM BASED ON SNOW AT LOUVICIENNES, BY A SISLEY

Thick path of snow,
High, enclosing walls.
Snow falling, constant, always.
Sinking sky, trees rise to meet it.
Whistling, wailing winds,
Trapped between walls.
Awkwardly moves a dark lady,
Crunching beneath her feet, compressed.
Cape of fur clothes her,
The icy breeze stings my eyes.

As the snow falls, constant, always.

Outside isolation,
Inside congregation,
Flames flicker.
Path of snow,
Blanket of cold,
The season takes hold.

Catherine Hale (17)
Haybridge High School

CIGARETTE

Poisonous smoke, flowing like a chimney,
riddled with chemicals, no one knows.
Yellow teeth, corroded, worn,
nicotine breath, stale and overpowering.

Volcano lava, hot and bright,
dirty ash rains on the floor.
Ashtrays overflowing,
like a running tap,
tar coating both your precious lungs.

A harmful drug, filthy and addictive,
constant damage to your body.
Chesty coughs, piercing pains,
heart attacks and cancer,
cigarettes are to blame.

Nigel Jones (18)
Haybridge High School

POEM BASED ON POSTCARD OF VASLAV NIYINSKY IN DANSE SIAMOISE FROM LES ORIENTALES

Lizard poised
Feet of pointed satin
Mouth open in anticipation
Black magic, cold enigma, conspicuous envy
Patterns interwoven on crusted silk
Skin iridescent
Watchful eyes
Hands beat a slow rhythm of thunder
The cascade of fabric on rock
Arrows of silver, shooting sharply
Poison ivy
I see a predator, eyes do not flicker
I see power
Curdled milk, frozen with breath
An angelic face - deception
Serpent smiles, royalty and wealth
Lizard poised
His stare concealed delight chilled
Power and darkness be killed

Gemma Clemson (17)
Haybridge High School

CAROUSEL

People upright,
> bold,
>> unmoved
horses mechanical jolt,
danger encouraging always.
Clasping clouds of darker blue
portrays abused screams
scaring,
> menacing,
>> tortured,
Straight lace - strong edge
Metal grinding cogs so near,
screams and joy removed
clustered bodies intertwined
moving - without cause,
danger encouraging always
candy sweet,
> fluffy soft,
along the hard rimmed fair,
bright - and - cold.
Hooves thundering.

Jody Neale (17)
Haybridge High School

THE FEATHER

A lone feather floating in the wind,
Darting movements as it flutters from gust to gust.
It softly settles on the ground
Alone.

Once it was part of a great wonder,
The plumage of a bird,
Now its beauty is singular
Yet still an object of interest.

Stephen Ford (18)
Haybridge High School

CATCHING STARS

Curving naked beauty
soft silk streaming
Pulling always
Darkness streaked
with threads of glistening silver.
Bold light
escapes underfoot.
A rustling swish
of silk on skin.
Brightness glinting
gleefully unnoticed.

I pity them,
their hopeless task
Pulling always.
Scentless air grows thick
All around darkness spreads
and light draws in.

Curving naked beauty,
Their hopeless fight
plunging the world into eternal night

Jenny Lowe (17)
Haybridge High School

THE BLACK SWAN

Body of the pond, the Sand Drudger
Lays moored in position
As it spades the pool floor.
Leaving seal fur on the surface
It forages for food beneath.

The red wine bottle cap rises
And the dragon wings extend
To reveal a cannonball chest

Once a cotton wool signet
Now - dark flying boat
Running for takeoff
In a watery shower.

The floating poison ivy's
Periscope stretches up then down.
Sucking food, the hoovering mouth
Glides across water
Honking warning to fellow seagoers.

The dark as death honesty
Adds to its sister's white purity.
But deception aids the pure
Yet the family's strength bears no difference.
The calm or storm of each image
Is decided by the viewer's vision.
The crystal ball perception
Lets us see what we want to see
Beauty or strength, purity or mystery.

The swan drudges on.

Alex Kyte (17)
Haybridge High School

THE PIGEON

Posture, strut, walk
Pose
Flitter, flutter, land
Pose
Fly a bit, wash a bit, squawk a bit
Pose
Challenging, fearless, arrogant
Stare
Little beady eyes
Stare
Waddle, wibble, wobble
Pose
Stop, stare.

Andrew Boynton (17)
Haybridge High School

DRIVE-THROUGH

When I am *drunk,*
I want to go to a drive-through,
Not in a car.
Just two in front and two behind
Maybe even a coach party!
The driver, me, winds down the 'window'
Asks for a Big Mac
            a hamburger
            large fries.
Our words are slurred
We try not to fall.
We try to stop laughing
We can't
'Please come again!'

Caroline Allison (18)
Haybridge High School

POEM

When I'm old

I wonder if in years to come
My favourite food will still taste nice
or if I'll wear similar clothes

Deep down I know things change
but ponder how my mind will think

Will my house be a bungalow down a quiet lane?
Or anything I can afford at the time -
whatever that may be

I say I won't be like Nan or Mom
But know it's fate for me.

Will I make sure I'm not like the rest
The hair cut, the make-up, the talk of youth
Or follow and shadow I think that the case.

Nicola Staples (17)
Haybridge High School

THE HAND

Starfish
Long,
reaching,
pale tentacles
protected by ruby coloured ovals

Imperfect
Childhood blemish
hiding behind a facade of metallic beauty.

Emma Sloper (17)
Haybridge High School

INDIAN EXOTIC

Stray release,
Undertoned order,
Indian exotic,
Egyptian water.

Close air,
Indifferent daylight,
Awaiting darkness,
Portrays insight.

Gentle traveller,
Mythical power,
Passionate strength,
A burning flower.

Pharaoh's daughter,
Golden maid,
Egyptian water
Absorbed always.

Passionate incense,
Cascade of chant,
Close air,
Indifferent daylight.

Golden maid,
Ivory content,
Smothered by,
Egyptian scent.

Charlotte Akers (18)
Haybridge High School

DIARY

I have your trust, your friendship
I know your innermost thoughts.
I've shared your wildest nights
and through your illness I've cared.

You've coveted,
You've sinned,
To that I'm testament,

I'm always there.

I may be thrown away.
Forgotten.
Lost without a care.

Yet I will remain faithful,
Where your soul was bared.

Gemma Porter (17)
Haybridge High School

DETAILS OF THE PICTURE
OF THE LADY OF SHALLOTT

Creaking wood, ageing boat
Virginal white, unmarked skin
Candle burning always
the gentle breeze
rushing through blood-red trees.
A knight - mighty white horse
ready to rescue fair maiden
The rushing cool water
caresses the ageing wood.
Red, golden, silver,
Knight's armour shining.

Bright dawn appears
Over the dark horizon.
Candle burning always
with the smell of scented wax.
Ahead, rippling waterfall
with water rushing fast.
Creaking wood, ageing boat
The lady doesn't care
as wind blows fine hair.

Liz Longden (17)
Haybridge High School

FRIENDS ALWAYS

Summer sun beats down on young bodies
flowers spread sweet perfumed spray,
friends,
always.
Murmurs mingle as one,
fertility blossoming.
Blinding - glint - metallic intruder.
Soft silk sways in the gentle breeze.
Glimpse of blinding falsity.
Now I, a ghostly figure, stand alone,
friends
always?
Still, no breeze, no pretty poppy's sweet
perfume.
They've gone,
we're no longer one.

Clare Hill (17)
Haybridge High School

FAIR ROSAMUND IMPRISONED

Watchman spies on auburn tresses
Her hands clasp in desperate longing
staring through windows of opportunity
always

The breeze lifts her veil
but inside is still, so still
the delicate rose creeps inside
clashing with gaudy fabrics
outside the mute river flows
flies hover above

Cut roses stand in a rounded vase
catching the little light on offer
I see the painting on the side
three men chivalrous in action
Staring through windows of opportunity
always
Fresh air perfumed with flowers

A man in a boat
A child on a bank
Watchman spies on auburn tresses
Armoured man carries shield
if only she was in the open field

Becky Wyatt (17)
Haybridge High School

FIGURE OF BALLET

Bound twine wrapped, boots.
Hill formed by curvature of knee.

Immense detail always,
a darkened room.
Cold like space, a void of darkness.
Tassel hangs like a string of vine,
jungle deep,
silence, white,
paints the floor.

Falling vines, like a river.
I hear and see damaged perfection,
only part reflection.

Immense detail always,
dust and smoke to be tasted.
Outside is death, war.

Cold like space, a void of darkness.
In this canopy of protection
rests a man of perfect correction.

Sam Zalin (18)
Haybridge High School

THE MIDNIGHT RIDE

The horse gallops through the darkness
At an outstanding speed.
With a boy on its back
Wishing to be free.
They go on and on, not stopping at all
To see if they are at the end of the world.

Polly James (9)
Hereford Cathedral Junior School

THE SEASONS

Spring is about new life,
Yellow daffodils bowing their trumpets,
Playful white lambs wagging their tails,
The birds building nests in the treetops,
And the gardeners planting bulbs and seeds.
          Waiting for . . .

Summer is the time for people to go on holiday,
And to go to the beach.
And of course the scent of roses in the air.
The fun of hay-making,
The noise of tractors fills the air
          Getting ready for . . .

Autumn is about the leaves changing colour on the trees,
About the trees dropping their leaves.
Sunflowers as tall as ever
Conkers falling to the ground.
People making jam and filling the freezer.
          Preparing for . . .

Winter is the time for great fun,
Tobogganing, building snowmen, and snowfights.
Animals hibernating.
Dark, cold, miserable nights.
Cosy by the log fire.
          Resting for . . .

Nicholas Barnett (10)
Hereford Cathedral Junior School

AN ORDINARY DAY

I always wake up late
And then I have to rush
And that is why I sometimes forget
To give my hair a brush.

I make my way downstairs
To have some tasty breakfast
Because I cannot go to school
Until I'm full at last.

I have to brush my teeth
To keep them nice and clean
And then I go and dress myself
Ready to be seen.

My mum takes us to school
And we are never late
We always have to stand outside
The entrance lobby gate.

I work so hard at school
As everyone will tell you
And then I go back home
To help my mum out too.

It soon is time for bed
And I go up the stairs
And dream of many days to come
When I have no more cares.

Becky Davidson (11)
Hereford Cathedral Junior School

An Autumnal View

A view of autumn is very strong.

The cathedral that has been through
so many autumns before this one.
And the trees that have thrown away
their leaves so many times.
The morning dew which will soon be frost.

The leaves rotten, once they have jumped
through the swimming pool of air.
They are dying with tawny, crimson and ochre colours.
Golden and jade are the colours
of the leaves still holding on.
The dazzling light of the sun making
the leaves grow and then letting them fall.

The leaves on the trees are
still in their thousands.
But all the leaves that have
fallen are russet with the dew.

Murray Warwick Jones (10)
Hereford Cathedral Junior School

Autumnal Beauty

One day in autumn I stepped outside,
And was hit by a magnificent radiant light of beauty.
A fantastic area of colour, pea-green, honey-yellow,
Flame-orange, scarlet-red, caramel-brown and
a monumental amount.
There was a magnitude of life
A massive amount of new smells, sounds and colour.

The next day I stepped outside and found
birds, hedgehogs, squirrels and much more.
All of the trees were going bare,
The leaves were on the floor if not on
their journey to the ground.
The fruit was ripe, the nuts were brown,
The conkers were ready.
And after the fun,
The next day it was gone.

James Sweetman (10)
Hereford Cathedral Junior School

THE MOON

His face grieves in sadness,
As he unwillingly shines,
I ask his night friends,
What is wrong,
but they say,
'We can't tell you.'
'Why is that?' I ask
Because he wants to keep it a secret.
'Please tell me,' I beg.
'Oh, all right then.'
Say his night friends.
'He says he is lonely and sad,
He says he is cold and tired
But he also says you are lucky
He can see you all night
He says you are warm and safe.'

Freya Don (9)
Hereford Cathedral Junior School

IT'S HARVEST TIME

It's harvest time
The fruits are ripe
The flowers have bloomed
And the leaves now fall

The crimson shines
Through the tree branches bare,
Conkers fall
From the trees of the field

You hear the children playing
And the ducks on the pond
Because it's harvest,
It's harvest time.

Thomas Spearing (10)
Hereford Cathedral Junior School

I WONDER

I wonder if I am I
Or what is what
If the world is great or small?

I wonder if we are alive or dead
Or even here at all.

I wonder if love is good or bad
Are we happy or are we sad?

I wonder if animals can speak and sing
Or always run around in rings?

I wonder if day could turn into night
Or always be dark or always be light?

I wonder if tomorrow will be good as today
Or will everything just fade away.

I wonder?

Eleanor J Steele (10)
Hereford Cathedral Junior School

AUTUMN TODAY

Autumn today,
Will blow the leaves my way,
The wind will blow,
ready for the winter with snow.

The swirling sky,
in the corner of your eye,
The feeling of insulation
and hibernation.

Harvest has drawn,
Taking its corn,
People giving,
with the feeling of living,
Summer will die,
and autumn will fly.

Charlotte Collings (10)
Hereford Cathedral Junior School

AUTUMN

As I stepped out of my house
Into the yard,
I smelled a sweet refreshing smell.
Birds chirping in the treetops.
I could see amethystine on a bush
Golden leaves
Falling down,
Olive bushes everywhere
I can smell freshly cut grass in the distance.
The leaves are brittle and hard.

That is my view of autumn.

Wil Clay (11)
Hereford Cathedral Junior School

AN ORDINARY DAY

I see the trees standing gnarled and old,
I see the leaves emerald, green and gold,

They crunch under my solid feet,
Have you tried the blackberries? They taste a treat.

I smell a wonderful woody smell,
Listen, I hear the church bell.

Oh, look, what can I see?
The river winding to the sea.

I looked into the gentle hill,
And saw my house waiting still.

Beth Healey (10)
Hereford Cathedral Junior School

MUM

My mother is the nicest one
And, to please her, my aim
Is, however cross she is
To love her just the same.

You might think 'I hate Mother!'
But she doesn't hate you
And, sooner or later
You'll feel that way too.

You might see my mum and think she's plain
But if you were me you'd think again.
For me it's the inside that counts
Not what you can see that's out.

Mum does the housework all day long
I offer to wash up,
But she says, 'There's no difference made
By plates and the odd cup.'

Mum washes the clothes
And she makes the food
If I were her I would be glad
It was for three and not a whole brood.

My dad, though, goes out shopping,
My mother does the rest.
If I see that she's distraught
I creep off and try not to be a pest
        Because
Mum, you really are
        The best!

Rosalind Higman (10)
Hereford Cathedral Junior School

AN ORDINARY DAY

As I walk home from school
I look into the sky
It is very dull and misty
Just about to burst with rain
When I walk on the pavement
Cars, lorries and buses whoosh past
Nearly knocking me over
Then it is quiet
Nothing to be seen
Just a few people in their houses
Watching the TV screen
Then a person walks past me
I look at him He has ragged clothes with holes
I'm wondering in my head
Did he choose to live like that
Or was he hard to live with and got kicked out
Then I reach my home
And have my tea.

William Spicer (10)
Hereford Cathedral Junior School

A HAUNTING DREAM

I walk mindlessly on broken glass splintered
upon a spiral staircase.
Treading hard on human dreams,
Killing all humanity; the insane.
I carry a burden; weightless is my mind.
Graciously I travel among luscious orchards
fruitful and bright, every smiling child's face
Is captured inside a shimmer of broken hazy glass.
I travel amongst landscapes carrying seasons' spice,
And turn my head. Glancing, gazing at stars,
To face the right; the sun, so far.
Falling into intense heat and flame,
I try to explain what visions I pursued
Could not prevent a stuttered remorse.
Swiftly, slowly, trading a worn already
trail of lilies, grass and hay,
weeping willows cried; bowed. I felt alone, scared.
Reversing my pace backwards through all my lives,
Naked I run, I am chased.
By the knife of human anxiety and angered growth.
My heart chased my feet, my soul was unseen.
Venturing abroad upon the wings of a swan
Pressured by reality's strife,
onwards unrealistically running; I trip and fall.
I float simultaneously into the unknown
my death; the hell.
I am now a different person awake.
I sweat the rain I feel pelt upon my breast,
As I fall, I fall, as I fall into death.

Emma Bacon (16)
Hereford Sixth Form College

TRANSFORMED

The earth beckons, as it always has,
to gaze out upon its beauty,
Shadows dance over shimmering fields,
Like a thousand reeds in a shining sea.
Hills, green and lush, stand
As friendly giants, to meet the crystal sky.
Scattered clouds swathe the sun,
Softening the brilliance of warming summer light.
Butterfly, on the other side,
emerges out of its cocoon.
Once drab caterpillar is shiny, bright, new,
Transformed it flies away, to meet destiny.
Turning into the darkest places, no escape for me,
Trapped by awkwardness and insecurity,
Wanting to fine peace from all that seems to be.
Earth expresses itself, in its entirety.
Free,
Like I want to be.

Sarah Featonby (15)
Hereford Sixth Form College

PARALYSIS

Dive head first into the depths of Desire.
What do you feel?
'Pain, Pleasure and a tingling of Lust.'

Sip the cool waters of Oblivion.
What do you taste?
'Uncertainty, a pinch of Pestilence and a dash of Despair.'

Stare through the infinite window of Eternity.
What do you see?
'Fear, Misery and, if I squint, Hope.'

Inhale the fragrance from this bottle of Conflict.
What do you smell?
'Discord, Hostility and a trace of Terror.'

Listen carefully to the melody of Belief.
What do you hear?
'Devotion, Hysteria and the low hum of Hypocrisy.'

Nene Harrison (17)
Malvern Girls' College

WHAT AM I?

Tall I stand on the edge of the cliffs,
towering over the sea,
shaped like a cylinder,
coloured like candy with a golden crown,
in summer I am visited by many,
and conquered by few,
who are rewarded with a well-earned view,
I feel happy within my sun-baked walls,
in winter with the people gone,
I face the tempest all alone,
trying to save friends from the great unknown,
by rotations within my golden crown.

I am a lighthouse!

Oliver William Croad (11)
Royal Grammar School, Worcester

FOOTBALL FEVER - IN THE MANNER OF BEOWULF

Spending soggy Saturdays supporting my team
Ninety nail-biting nervous minutes until the end.
The teams thunder towards the pitch
Practising perfect passes, putting penalties past the post.
A ridiculous referee runs round and round.
The whistle blows, two teams take their places,
Chosen captains confront capable competitors.
The ball blasts back and forth,
Terrifying tackles taken by dirty defenders.
Frantic forwards force menacing moves.
Suddenly, someone sees space before the goal
Carefully crosses creating a chance,
The goalie grunts and groans,
Crowds cheering the greatest goal.

Matthew Steele (11)
Royal Grammar School, Worcester

THE GERBIL

I am very small and furry,
cuddly as can be.
I love my sunflower seeds,
I dig tunnels inside my cage,
and I love to come out and play.
I run around very fast,
and I love my owner too,
and I love being a gerbil.

Alexander Chew (11)
Royal Grammar School, Worcester

MY ANGLO-SAXON RIDDLE

Shot at many times, but never killed.

Hit, chopped and chipped at,
Never thrown.

A man's only saviour.

Bloody and messy,
Yet polished and oiled.

Braided in gold.

It spends its time counting its wounds,
As many men carry it to their death.

Tom Spaughton (11)
Royal Grammar School, Worcester

MY ANGLO-SAXON RIDDLE

I have a long, rough, snake-like body.
I am a slayer of slaves.
Every man hates my crack
My long thin body slashing slow
Scandalous strokes
When resting I curl up in solemn
Silence.

What am I?

Whip!

Christopher Hobbs (11)
Royal Grammar School, Worcester

At The Soccer Match - In The Manner Of Beowulf

The soccer star, sliding snake-like
Through the defence, dived dubiously
Causing the crowd to yell.

The reds and the greens with supporters as well
Grappled to the ground near the goalmouth
As the flabby fists fell.

The referee, raining red cards by now,
Was waving the play to go on
And Frankie's figure darted past

And the drunk dribbled the ball.
He skilfully swerved past the spectators
Thinking his team would score at last.

The goalmouth grew, and great Frankie
Blasted the ball toward the back of the net
And the goalie, gasping, grappled his way to the line.

The ball fizzled through the stunned spectators
As the goalie ran raggedly to his right.
Would he get there on time?

And the ball wavered well wide from its path
Causing the keeper to crumble to the ground.
Then Frankie got his bearings.

The grizzly green's goal was at the other side of the ground
And the shot he had own-goaled was true!
He shouldn't have been so daring.

But suddenly Smith saw the scene:
The red player rushed roaring
'Get outta my way!'

And dived daredevil right across the reds' goal,
Headed the ball outward and saved the day.

And with the goal kick the reds scored. *Hooray!*

Edward Millington (11)
Royal Grammar School, Worcester

THE BLITZ - IN THE MANNER OF BEOWULF

As the terrifying thunder taunted the people below,
German bombers flew fiercely above.
Then the bombers let go their dangerous and dauntless bombs.
Down below, people were already in their dark, dull shelters.
They listened carefully for the bombers to go.
All of a sudden, the raging flames burst through bolted door,
Then deadly silence.
All that could be heard was the furious flames that had killed
                                                    many people,
But that was another violent, vicious bombing over.
The next could be worse,
This frightening, ferocious war was far from over.

Russell Morriss (12)
Royal Grammar School, Worcester

AN ANGLO-SAXON RIDDLE

Elegantly I jump up high and dive down into water wet
And come back up with prey in mouth
Oh how beautiful am I!
I fly across the lake - to where I live
And drop my prey down on the floor
Then I go back to the lake long
And spot my prey again and dive down
The water wet passes through me as I catch him
The biggest I have ever had
Oh I am the most beautiful of living things.
Who am I?

Kingfisher!

Adam Callaghan (11)
Royal Grammar School, Worcester

MY ANGLO-SAXON RIDDLE

I am made of metal.
When I start I make a roar.
Eyes like a glowing light.
My name is on a little plastic board.
I usually have seats and a wheel.
I blow out smoke from my back.
When I stop two red lights
go on then off.
You have to pull a stick up
or I roll away.
Now I stay until another day.

Matthew Jones (11)
Royal Grammar School, Worcester

SPELLBOUND

Darkness swirling upon moonlight,
Star encrusted carapace,
Burn my eyes a million times,
As I observe my inner space.

In highest tower of citadel,
Bound heavy tome on dusty shelf.
Is set in print of golden leaf,
The darkest wisdom; mine to keep.

Within the symbol on the floor
Five points in chalk, no less, no more,
To bind my spirit to my bone
While travelling the demon zone.

I stand controlled, while summoning,
My guide in darkness, screaming thing,
With taloned claw and sabre fang,
It leads me through this strangest land.

Observe with me, come, watch a while,
The world inside me as I smile,
The smile of evil, the leer of death,
The howling beast with blackest breath.

For in my folly of arrogant faith,
I lost my soul to a demon wraith.
To the end of time I stand my ground
In my self-made prison, I am spellbound.

Mark Caseley (12)
St John's CE Middle School

SPELLBOUND

A dark black spinning hole
Sucking things in.
A speechless part of nature,
That no one begins.
It starts from one tiny star,
Then there's a horrific bang!
A strong suction starts spinning, pick up light,
Planets,
And whole entire galaxies!
Scientists become speechless,
Over things like that.
But I become spellbound, over phenomena like that!
Why it sucks in light,
And defeats all gravity.
That's another question.
Because all I want to know is why it's there
And what is at the end.

Timothy Maughan (12)
St John's CE Middle School

MY FELINE FRIEND

My adventure seeking cat,
Crawls through the undergrowth,
She's like a miniature wildcat,
Stalking her unsuspecting prey,
She pauses,
She's ready,
She springs on a basking fly,
But she's not victorious,
That's my cat!

My cat lies,
In the cool morning light,
What's that noise?
She thinks,
She hears a rustle, crunch, crunch,
My cat gets up,
But she's tired and weak,
It's early morning it's only the dog,
That's no contest,
That's my cat!

Anna Ostrowski (11)
St John's CE Middle School

MEDITERRANEAN MELODY

I gazed upon the water's surface,
Transfixed by the outstanding colour,
The water lapped around sun browned ankles,
It was warm and soothing.

Small shoals of fish swam past me,
Whilst brushing against my leg,
A whole new world lay before me,
It was so tranquil.

I was dazed,
A spell had been cast upon me,
It was wonderful,
Never before had I been so enchanted.

Eleanor Morgan (12)
St John's CE Middle School

THE GHOST OF THE CHILD

In the attic of that very old house,
in the dead of night is a ghost.
The ghost belongs to a child, so small,
that haunts the attic of that very old house.

The attic door swings open then closes.
Nobody enters and nobody comes out of the
attic of that very old house.

The ghost of the child haunts its parents at the
dead of night,
it haunts the attic of that very old house.

The ghost of the child was set free at last,
it no longer haunts the attic of that very old house.

Catherine Furey (12)
St John's CE Middle School

MASON

I remember when I first got on a horse,
scared and all alone.
so high from the ground, so spellbound.

Trotting along on the open ground, round
and round, up and down, spellbound.

I love my horse, he's so stunning in every simple way,
his forelock, his mane, his beautiful cain,
oh he makes me spellbound.

It's time to go home, so please don't moan,
My beauty, my precious, my spellbound
Mason.

Christine Weston (12)
St John's CE Middle School

DOLPHIN FUN

Mischievous creatures of the sea,
Roaming around so happily.
Hiding below the waters deep,
Waiting to make their graceful leap.
Teasing humans in their boats,
Anxious for a glimpse of glossy coats.

Suddenly the sea is still,
They've sped away to make their kill.
Shoals of fish ventured near,
Never again to reappear.
Soft sounds of joy echo around,
The family group is safe and sound.

Holly Maund (11)
St John's CE Middle School

SPELLBOUND

In the showroom bright and gleaming
all shiny red and chrome.

From its leather seat and its jet black fairing
to its gleaming paint job that it was wearing.

I stand and gaze and look with wonder and
hope I someday own.

This beautiful BMW bike, a joy to ride alone.

Ashley Rollings (12)
St John's CE Middle School

THE ROLLER-COASTER

I stood there waiting all alone, waiting anxiously.
I saw the people high above staring down at me.
I wondered what it would be like to be so incredibly high.
See if it would be good or not to be high up in the sky.

I finally got to the front of the queue, all excitedly.
I sat down ready to go with no one beside me.
There was a sign of movement, we were off and ready to go,
Climbing up the big steep hill it was now time to hold on.

We started to go round,
Ready to go down this big, steep hill,
Frightened but ready to go, thinking,
What it would be like to go down this big steep hill.

Soon the ride was over, it was a brilliant sight,
To be back down from out of the sky,
Back down to the sweet light,
I stepped out of the cart . . . *Spellbound*!

Lisa Mills (12)
St John's CE Middle School

SPELLBOUND

He's a prisoner waiting to be sentenced,
As she makes him play this waiting game
Sometimes he feels like going insane,
Spellbound!

She sends his mind into a whirl,
Just over simple little things
As he's left waiting for the phone to ring,
Spellbound!

He's like the prey she never catches,
He always has to be on guard,
No one told him this could be so hard,
Spellbound!

And yet through all the hurt he doesn't care,
Even if their future looks quite dim,
All this because she makes him
Spellbound!

Jennifer Macdonald (12)
St John's CE Middle School

A WISH UPON WISHES

A distressed mother talks to me on the telephone,
Explains her child's illness.
To my alarm all fears are confirmed,
This mortal illness is cancer.

No one can believe such a dreadful thing,
Could happen to Hazel.
At the age of four with her life ahead,
How cruel it may be for her life may just pass by.

With her long blonde locks which cascaded
around her face,
Before her last prayer, her last hope is chemotherapy,
Now her beautiful face has only tears to frame it.
I'm afraid she knows she has not long to live.

I reach out to the little girl I have loved and I have known,
With a fire in my heart called hope.
I wish upon wish for a spell which will bind and
keep her with me, not in spirit but in life.

Kayleigh Pearson (12)
St John's CE Middle School

FEAR

Shadows,
Deep, dark and dreamless
Figures
Huddled in spaces
Inhabited by ghosts
From a past
Littered with questions

Dreams,
Short, sharp and vivid
Scenes
Flickering in sepia
Unloved in truth
It's a fear
Scattered with anger

What is my fear?
Behind locked doors
Storms,
Twisters,
Shadowy movements
In the slightest of light

Some say
Fear is the key
But is it the key to my life . . . ?

Jolene Nutting (11)
St John's CE Middle School

SPELLBOUND

The attendance at a football match
Was like some strange sort of catch
In the terraces, people roaring with great sound
And it seemed as if the match was spellbound.

There was a player on the pitch, loved by all spectators
'His skills are absolutely breathtaking' said the commentator
In the terraces, people jeering him with great sound
And it seemed as if the player was spellbound.

There was a referee on the pitch, loved by all spectators
'He keeps coming in for those rough tackles' said the commentator
In the terraces, people jeering him with great sound
And it seemed as if the player was spellbound.

There was a referee on the pitch, loved by all spectators
'Doing his job as perfect as a calculator' said the commentator
In the terraces, people cheering him with great sound
As he sends off the tough tackling player
And it seemed as if the incident was spellbound.

There had just been a goal on the pitch, loved by some spectators
'A beautiful goal into the top corner' said the commentator
In the terraces, people cheering and jeering the goal scorer
with great deafening sound
And it seemed as if the goal was spellbound.

Sam Flory (12)
St John's CE Middle School

LONELINESS

The tears that flow will never stop
The wounds will never heal
The flowers spread across the ground
Just proves that it is real

Our pain, our heartache, our sorrow so
Great, a part of us all died that week
Diana Queen of Hearts her eyes so blue
And deep, so innocent her smile
So bright her hair so light

But upon a night it came to an end
The joy, the laughter, replaced by tears
and torture.

Diana, Princess of Wales no longer
laughs and smiles but is instead in the
greatest joy of them all
Where she can laugh and smile again
But this time her happiness can last forever.

Annabel Webb (11)
St John's CE Middle School

SPELLBOUND

In the darkness late at night
a tiger lies watching

The lights shimmer shadows onto the tents
where people shiver in their beds

Men with guns assure them that the tiger will not attack
hopefully tomorrow the tiger will not be back

In the morning, sunny and bright, the men go searching

Walking slowly gun in hands, the men go forth in a foreign land

The tiger attacks throwing a man to the floor
a gun shot is heard the tiger falls dead on the floor.

Aimeé Rollings (12)
St John's CE Middle School

SPELLBOUND!

There it is, above my house,
Flying through the black night sky.
Whenever I see it I stop and think,
'How did it get there, and why?'
I stare at it, this burning ball,
I'm hypnotised by its white light.
I step outside and realise,
It has a tail, burning bright.
This comet, travelling through the sky,
High above the planet Earth,
You incredible chunk of black space rock,
Who or what gave you birth?
Oh, Hale-Bopp, (this is the comet's name)
I know you don't appear for long,
but why don't you stay with us on Earth?
We humans have nothing wrong.
Hale bop, why do you leave us now?
We await your return,
When you come again we shall have advanced,
And more about you we will learn.

Samir Hissaund (12)
St John's CE Middle School

MY BROTHER DAVE

Here I sit in my home,
I am sad and all alone,
My brother has left,
Now he has gone,
He has gone to live with his
best friend John

All alone in my big empty house,
With no one to talk to
But my pet mouse,
No one to turn to, no one to care,
No one to play with, no one to share

I look at photos of my brother Dave,
And all the presents and cards that he gave,
I wish my brother would come home soon,
So he could put an end to my gloom.

Natalie Duce (11)
St John's CE Middle School

GAMBLER

My friends all nab the jackpot,
And yes they always win!
But me, I spend my money,
And chuck it in the bin!

Yesterday I went to town,
To go to the arcade!
People walking in and out,
I joined the big parade!

Men in suits were laughing,
As I spent my £1.02!
I even went as far as selling,
My super Nike Air shoes!

My friends all think I'm nutty,
Especially my friend Josh!
But now I've learnt my lesson,
And I've got loads of dosh!

Kris Brown (12)
St John's CE Middle School

SPELLBOUND

They threw me out, without a doubt,
For hunger, loss and life.
I'm ever decreasing, my life is a sin,
For what could I do that would ever make change?
I had no choice in either range.
I had to go!
Leave far from this weird and mysterious clove of bewilder.
I walked scowl faced to the station.
Memories of love, gifts and excitement, specified in my mind,
But that wasn't coming my way.
What was my life to become of?
How was I to survive?
No one seemed to be on my side.
Isolated in my own emotions.
I was twelve, and could have had a life of fantasy,
but I had nothing, and had to die.

Laura Stickley (12)
St John's CE Middle School

GYMNASTICS

I was afraid and worried
I can't do all these things.
My heart pounded more
and more watching the splits
on the floor.

I tried the rings, the horse
and the beam, they all looked
easy but not what they seemed.

I tried the crab and the back flip too.
My handstands are rubbish but my
cartwheels will do.

In front of the crowd I'm spellbound.
I look at them, they look at me,
we joined together instantly.

The day is over, I feel so tired,
they all said goodbye and
see you tomorrow.

My heart is pounding more and more,
just can't wait to get on that
bouncy floor.

Stacey Baker (12)
St John's CE Middle School

MY GRAN

There she sat in her chair
Her hands lay by her side as she stared
lifelessly into the air.

I look at her
she looked at me
she had a twinkle in her eye
and so, very carefully, I walked up beside
Her and gave her a kiss
I gave her some grapes and so she ate.

I looked at her
she looked at me
so spellbound.

She is dead now
vanished into thin air
but when I'm sat alone
somehow I know she's there.

There she sat in her chair
her hands lay by her side
As she stared lifelessly into the air
so spellbound.

Christy Archer (12)
St John's CE Middle School

SPELLBOUND

Every time I dance I'm under my own spell,
And capture the audience with my spell,
Every flawless movement I make,
The audience is captivated with every step I take.

Under a spell I leap across the floor,
Lost in my own world once more,
Who notices me out of breath,
As long as I perform my best.

And in the twirls and leaps and bounds,
To the music and the sound,
I leave the stage,
Completely spellbound.

Michelle Heeley (12)
St John's CE Middle School

SPELLBOUND

I am spellbound over you,
I would rue the day I met you,
If you asked me to.

I am spellbound over you,
I would leave with you,
If you asked me to.

I am spellbound over you,
I would wilt away
If you died,
Without me, by your side.

Daniel Bate (12)
St John's CE Middle School

THE FISHERMAN'S GHOST

I was walking my dog, one November night,
down on the beach, in a pale moon light.

When out on the pier, there appeared a glow,
moving, moving, slow, slow.

The glow was a fisherman, with a torch shining ahead,
both my dog and I watched with dread.

It was a ghost, sure to be, straight through him,
I could see the sea.

I could not move, although I tried, the dog whimpered,
by my side.

A gust of wind, made me shiver, the ghost disappeared
with a quiver.

The very next day, at first day light, I made a call,
to Mr Cartwright.

He agreed to meet me, on the pier, to tell me what,
I needed to hear.

Fred went out fishing, on his own, while his wife,
waited at home.

His boat crashed, against the rocks, he floated back,
in towards the docks.

From that night, he walked the pier, looking for his wife,
called Lier.

Louise Fuller (12)
St John's CE Middle School

NIGHTMARE OF THE SOUL

My dream began
And my heart slowed,
Beating to the rhythm of time.

I was engulfed in
The pleasure of my imagination,
And my mind was taken
Over by thoughts and meanings.

Overpowered by what was happening,
Unable to realise
That this power was death.

My dream deepened,
And now I could not escape.
My existence was stolen,
My last breath, released.

My dream revealed a fear,
That I now faced.

No longer a dream of meaning
but a nightmare of the soul.

Bonnie Heath (11)
St John's CE Middle School

A WINTER'S NIGHT

At the dead of night,
No sight to see,
The moon so bright,
It dazzled me,

The hooting owl,
The frozen water,
Spooky ghosts upon the water,

Sleeping animals,
begin to wake,
because the dawn,
Of Christmas day,

At the dead of night,
No sight to see,
The moon so bright,
It dazzled me.

Catherine Luke (12)
St John's CE Middle School

LANDING

A gentle movement to the right
Has the engine changed its tone
Or have my ears popping deceived me?
Is this the beginning of descent
Cabin crew scuttle round, tidying away my
tray table
Looking out, clouds are rushing past
I can just see the ground
My ears are popping once again
As we tilt to the right
A thump! A bump!
The undercarriage is locked in place
The Captain gives his final orders to the
cabin crew
'Doors to manual' and 'crew to landing positions'
From my window, houses and cars grow bigger
I can see the people
the ground comes closer and closer
Another bump and a rush of engine sound
We are down, and there's no more excitement.

James Phillips (12)
St John's CE Middle School

SPELLBOUND

The pain has just begun,
But still I live in hope,
If I can't break the spell,
I don't know how I'll cope.

The pain is getting worse,
So I have to shed a tear,
No longer can I withstand it,
The worry, the strife, the fear.

The pain will soon be over,
And then I'll be able to tell,
Of how I lived my life,
And how I broke the spell.

Alison Common (12)
St John's CE Middle School

WHITE WINTER'S WEASEL

White winter's weasel,
Darting through the snow,
Its feet small and padded,
Reflexes fast never slow.

An owl seeking prey,
In flight, strong with might
Landing on a branch
The weasel in its sight.

The owl swoops down silently
The weasel in surprise stilled
A feast for the carnivore
The weasel is killed.

Ben Taylor (12)
St John's CE Middle School

SPELLBOUND (THE UNIVERSE)

The Universe,
It has no end,
I wonder how,
It looks right now.
It has no floor,
Or ceiling, or door.
I wonder how,
It looks right now.
It has the sun, the moon, the stars
And all the Milky Way,
Galaxies, black holes and us.
I wonder how,
It looks right now.
How big would you have to be
If you were to see
The Universe?

Katie Chandler (12)
St John's CE Middle School

SPELLBOUND - BY THE SUN

Rising over in the east,
Orange, yellow and red.
Slowly rising till up high,
Shining warmly on the world below.
And then again sinking slowly down,
As the night draws near.
Setting over in the west,
Your beautiful colours,
Orange, yellow and red.

Laura Skirving (12)
St John's CE Middle School

SPELLBOUND BY FOOD

Help me, help me,
Please, please.
I need some food,
(anything but peas).
They bring me out in a horrible rash,
Oh forget it,
Just give me some cash.

I want some food,
I need it to live.
Anything will do,
Just give, give, *give!*

I'm desperate for food,
Give me some please.
If you don't know what to give me,
My favourite is cheese.

Oh please,
I don't like to beg.
But if you don't give me food,
I'll have to eat my own leg.

Alex Jordan (12)
St John's CE Middle School

SPELLBOUND

Watching a squirrel on the lawn,
Watching the sun rise up at dawn,
Looking at a baby lamb new-born.
These things leave me spellbound.

The lovely smell of fish and chips,
A model made of Lego bricks,
Watching a magician do his tricks.
These things leave me spellbound.

Seeing a helicopter rise above the wall,
When silky-white snow starts to fall,
The biggest Christmas present of them all.
These things leave me spellbound.

A steam train as it passes by,
Fireworks exploding in the sky,
Waves that crash and splash up high.
These things leave me spellbound.

James Page (11)
St John's CE Middle School

COLD IS . . .

Cold is the graveyard when you walk in it at night
Cold is an empty house, without any light.

Cold is when you step out of a bubbly warm bath
Cold is a child without a laugh.

Cold is a high up, marble shelf
Cold is a sad feeling inside yourself.

Cold is a swimming pool on a hot summer's day
Cold is an orphan without a home to stay.

Cold is milk and freezing ice-cream
Cold is the water of a mountain stream.

Cold is the white wilderness of the glistening snow
Cold is the shrill call of the jet black crow.

Cold is a wicked icy stare
Cold is a dead rabbit, fox or hare.

Cold is cobwebs sparkling on a winter's morn
Cold is the first light of the world at dawn.

Rebekah Lane (11)
St John's CE Middle School

SPELLBOUND

Focus.
Where is it?
There
Shhh.
Creeping, slowly, quietly, carefully,
Through the ever-dry grass.

Getting closer
Shhh, you might scare it.
Snap
Scamper, run, dash, quick.

Where did it go?
Focus.
There it is!
Slouching while closing in.
Closer, closer.
Stop, shhh.

Get ready,
Go, action.
Run, run, faster, quick.
Catching up and getting closer to the prey.
Pounce!
Just as I woke up.

Freja Dommett (12)
St John's CE Middle School

MY CAT

My cat is lovely,
Soft and cuddly,
My cat is perfect,
Bouncy and bubbly.

My cat don't scratch,
And my cat don't claw,
He's got a favourite patch,
And he's not allowed next door.

My cat is sweet,
He's cute and enjoys meat,
My cat is wonderful,
He's the cat you should meet.

My cat don't scratch,
And my cat don't claw,
He's got a favourite patch,
And he won't break the law.

My cat is black,
And he likes to roll on his back.
My cat is fabulous
And he don't smoke 'crack'.

Rachel Smith (11)
St John's CE Middle School

THE LIGHT OF DOOM

The boy silently waits alone;
Spellbound is he . . .
Watching, looking, staring, observing,
As the bulging light brightens.

The boy follows the light;
Fascinated and enchanted is he . . .
He can never walk straight into the light,
He walks and walks until, he eventually . . . *falls.*

Down and down he goes;
Scared and puzzled is he . . .
He screams as he falls,
Down, down, deep down, into a big dark pit.

Rats nibble at his fingers and toes;
Non-moving is he . . .
He's broken his back,
A bear tears away at his flesh.

He's a gonner!
Unconscious is he . . .
A lion chews his internal organs,
Blood seeps out onto the cold stone floor of the pit.
May he rest in peace!

James Bennett (12)
St John's CE Middle School

SPELLBOUND

They moved to the side,
To let him pass,
The poor, wrinkled man in his wheelchair.
A little girl looked up,
Looked up,
Spellbound.

He could feel her eyes at the back of his head,
Watching his every move.
Turning his head,
Slowly,
She was spellbound.

He tried to get through to her,
To make her understand,
But he could only flick weak hands in the air,
Trying,
Trying,
But spellbound.

Hannah Griffiths (12)
St John's CE Middle School

SPELLBOUND BY LOVE

I watch him here, I watch him there.
He's in my dreams at night.
Oh why can't I meet him?
Oh why oh why can't I be there with him?
He has a special place in my heart forever and forever.
I have his pictures in my room, I stare at them all night.
I love him now, I'll love him forever, forever, forever.

Katie Hagan (12)
St John's CE Middle School

THE PEOPLE'S PRINCESS

Shocking news came with the morning light,
Princess Diana died last night,

We all said this cannot be true,
But very soon the whole world knew,

Disbelief soon turned to tears,
People cried whatever their years,

No one could have thought,
The nation would be so distraught,

A scent of flowers filled the air
All of them placed with love and care,

The day soon came to say 'Goodbye'
Everyone watched with a tear in their eye,

Then total silence all around,
Not a single soul made a sound,

Far too soon out of sight,
To the People's Princess we say
'Goodnight.'

Kerry Monaghan (11)
St John's CE Middle School

SNOW SPELL

Drifting, silently dancing,
Twirling towards a blanketed earth.
Swirling, like the children of angels
Watched from a wintry window-glow.

Appearing from a milky sky,
Vanishing into an ice-cold quilt.
Hypnotic in their dreamy journey
Followed by eyes, alight with wonder.

Settling upon a cold, crisp mattress,
Icily warming the flowers beneath,
Endless in their magical frost-fleets
They hold every child under their spell.

Dreamt of by a thousand sleepers
Wished for in a thousand prayers,
Watched through frosty glazed over glass
Holding every glistening eye spellbound.

Siân Narsingh (12)
St John's CE Middle School

SMOKE

Smoke haunts you everywhere you go,
On top of the sheets and down below,
A smear on someone's face as they blow,
The steaming smoke rises with a flow.

With its ghastly smell and its deadly touch,
No wonder people hate it so much,
But no one has complained as such.

From the autumn bonfires see the smoke trail,
In the other gardens and up the vales,
            The smoke surrounds
                  my eyes.

Nikki Edwards (11)
St John's CE Middle School

SPELLBOUND

S he smiled that special smile,
P ictured in my dreams,
E specially when she's happy,
L ife is what it means.
L ittle, lovely and soft,
B ethany is her name,
O ften she would giggle,
U ntil we did the same.
N ow I see her smiling face,
D elightful, happy, full of grace!

Lisa Edge (12)
St John's CE Middle School

PEOPLE

Some people are fat,
Some people are thin,
Some people get bullied,
For the colour of their skin.
In our world people fight,
In our world people play,
But everybody dies at the end of the day.
No matter if you're fat,
No matter if you're thin,
It doesn't matter about your skin.
Please don't fight just get along,
For life is short but the road is long,
We will meet again just wait and see,
In Heaven together you and me.

Sophie Davies (12)
The Minster College

THOMAS THE BAD

I know a little boy called Thomas,
Who drives me up the wall,
Round the bend,
Till an everlasting end,
He's always playing with that ball.

He should be doing things so good,
And even though he knows he should,
Be doing things that are so good,
He goes downstairs in the night,
Just to give his mum a fright.
He ties the cat onto a kite,
And sends her up right out of sight!
He always creeps into my room,
And hits me with a great big spoon.
He does not mean to hurt me though,
'Cos I know he loves me so . . .
                    He's my brother!

Emma Savagar (11)
The Minster College

WITCHES

With pointed hats,
And bright black cats,
Fingers knobbly and bent,
They'll be after you with no delay,
The witches are here,
And here to stay!
With broomstick bold,
And eyes so bright,
Meeting them will give you a fright!

Natalie Hanson (11)
The Minster College

NO ONE KNOWS

Once there was a little boy
Who had a grisly, gruesome toy
It was five feet something tall
And as bouncy as a ball

It was red, blue-black and green
And if you squeezed it, it would scream
It could run around, around
And it only cost a pound

It would bounce up on the bed
And its name was great big Ed
Towards the mirror it would pose
But what it was no one knows.

Rosalyn Buckley (11)
The Minster College

FISHING

I love fishing
I go every week
Saturdays and Sundays
Cast
Caught in the sycamore tree
'Try again' says Smith
Laughing as much as he can
finally I get out
Raving river rod comes off the straight stand
'A six-pounder' I say.

Dane Baxter (13)
The Minster College

THE FIELD

He walks through the frightening field like a ghost
He cannot bear to get to the end
He wants to stop as he knows it's like
A lost world unknown to anyone else

He cannot bear to carry on as the tree
Is like a person swaying in the wind
A piece of thin wire sounding
Like a loud and sharp whistle of the wind
Through the tiny crack in the wall

He can hear noises like footsteps brushing the grass
So frightened to look behind just in case
There is someone following him like a stalker
Following someone.

He can walk faster and faster
But he would still feel frightened
And if there was a person behind him
They could walk faster and faster
So nothing would be gained

But it could be in his mind like a dream
Or made up by his imagination

If he gets to the bottom of the field
It will be like nothing happened
It would be like a dream forgotten about.

Anthony Price (13)
The Minster College

HECTOR THE COLLECTOR

Hector the collector
Was a really weird man,
He liked collecting bits and bobs,
Excepting old tin pans.
Collecting buckets he liked most,
(It was his speciality!)
But matchsticks came in second best,
(They were useful in reality)
He collected buckets of
Any shape,
Any size,
Any age,
Any colour,
From any place,
It just had to be a bucket!
When once a year his friends came round,
He'd send them where they couldn't be found,
Knowing as soon as they saw his rooms,
They would definitely not delay to say,
'You really should throw some of this
Revolting stuff away!'

Tess Eaton (11)
The Minster College

THE OWL

Fluffy the wonderful owl
Flies through the night.
He stalks all the little creatures
That come out in the moonlight.

His sweet voice carries through
The woods into the darkness.
The stars fade and the moon goes down
While the owl flies back to its h*ome.*

Terri Thwaites (11)
The Minster College

SPELLBOUND!

My old home is now a lonely cottage.
I go in, nothing is the same.
The lightening flashes through each window.
The thunder shakes the house.
The rain comes in through the holes in the roof.
I panic, the house crumbles.
My old room is wrecked.
My favourite picture comes down in front of me and cracks.
I have to leave.
I go into my mum and dad's room.
The funny posters on the door are ripped.
The wind blows them away.
Sad memories come back.
I can't stay any longer.
I have to go.
I rush out.
I turn back.
I stand spellbound.
My house slowly collapses.
'No,' I cry, 'It's gone.'
The rain makes me cry.
I wish I could have stayed longer.
That was my last *'Goodbye!'*

Jemma Price (11)
The Minster College

THE CARETAKER

Mr Jenkins kept the school
clean neat and tidy
But deep inside the boiler room
He kept lots of knives and forks
He also kept all the naughty children there
And also hundreds of dirty bottles and corks
Old tyres not a single wall was bare
Thousands of old broken pencils, rubbers and old
cracked glasses.
Old smelly socks and bent keys from all the many classes
One day the headteacher found him dead
Squashed flat under an old bed.

Danny Bufton (12)
The Minster College

THE DOLPHINS

Dolphins glide through the water,
like a torpedo,
Skin so soft and shiny,
A nose so long, but they do
not tell lies,
They splash and jump full of life,
Their friend, the whale, so big and strong,
They swim and swim no batteries needed,
The sun is setting, down and down,
No more swimming until tomorrow,
Our little friend says goodbye!

Colleen Morris (11)
The Minster College

THE MOTOR BIKE MAN

His hands are like tyres, covered with dirt,
The sound of his bike, which makes me alert.
His crystal blue eyes, not hidden away,
By the helmet he wears, to keep danger at bay.

His distinctive smile and bleached blond hair,
As bright as the light that keeps drivers aware.
His bike is the shade of a silk red rose,
The thorns are for danger, the colours for show.

But the power that he handles, the speed he takes on,
Won't compare to my feelings, they are just as strong.
He's what I like, he's one of a kind,
A motor bike man, I can't keep off my mind.

Rebecca Turner (16)
The Minster College

THE SQUIRREL

Furry little squirrel
Runs to collect nuts.
Bushy little tail swinging in the air.

Little paws climbing the tree trunks
Red as a rose shining in the sun.
Back home to store the nuts
Ready for winter.

In the night, sound asleep
No running or climbing trees
Till morning comes.

Lauren Skyrme (11)
The Minster College

PRINCESS DIANA

Diana Princess of the People
You have only been gone a few days
Yet already the world's been missing you
In hundreds and hundreds of ways.

A smile a touch of love you gave
That helped to ease their pain away
The price you have had
To show this world
Of ours today.

No matter the creed or the colour
No matter how well or how ill
You really cared about people
So people care for you still.

In person *Diana* may now be gone
But tomorrow and forever
Her memory lives on.

Victoria Jones (13)
The Minster College

A TREASURE COLLECTOR

My best friend is a collector
He's been collecting all his life
From football stickers to wagon wheels
And a very sharp carving knife
He's also got a battery powered football game
But he is often a great big pain
And all his plates are greasy
I'm glad I've got him as a friend
Because anyone else would drive me round the bend.

Martin Winney (11)
The Minster College

SPOILT ROTTEN

There once was a girl
Whose dad was an Earl
And she was spoilt rotten

She had a dream
She was covered in cream
And her dad said it was cotton

She thought he was right
So she took a big bite
Because she had forgotten

She cried and she cried
So her dad went and buyed
Some loo roll for her bottom.

Kirsty Lee Maund (11)
The Minster College

HECTOR THE COLLECTOR!

My best friend's called Hector,
And he's a spectacular collector,
He's got rats' tails like old hay bales,
Spooky stories and long long tales,
Cat flaps big bats,
Massive cats with little mats,
A massive book of nasty tricks,
A giant bowl of pick-up sticks,
Things that look and things that stare,
A massive bowl of underwear.
I know that I am Hector's friend,
But I think he's going round the bend!

Kirsty Burnside (11)
The Minster College

Mr Clopter That Mad Doctor

Mr Clopter
Was a mad doctor
He was also a collector
Of hearts that still beat
Eyes that still blink
Legs that still run
Hands that still grab
And lungs that still breathe
Noses that still sniff
The claws of a slink
The jaws of a sliff
Poor little animals such as
Rabbits and hamsters
Terrible creatures such as
Kronks and krankers
Four-eyed scroths and no-eyed scronkers
And the eyes and mouth
of a slaloo
All he needs now is
 You!

Luke Moran (11)
The Minster College

Swimmer

I know a little dog
Who thinks he is a frog
He kicks his back legs out
Just like a swimmer
He entered the Olympics
And now he is a winner.

Rosanna Plowman (11)
The Minster College

DIFFERENT

I'd like to be different.
Well-known
And popular.

All I am is boring
And horrible.
No one cares about my feelings,
Just how to upset me.

If I was different,
People might like me.
I am about as boring as it gets.

So if I had a wish
I would be different.
Better at work
And popular with people.

I would not know how to change
Or be different.
So I will have to live life the way I am.

Jody Broderick (14)
The Minster College

ANYWHERE

I would like to cast a spell upon me
to take me anywhere,
At first I'd go to Australia to see the koala bears,
I'd then go to Africa to see the tigers run,
And then I'd end up in Holland and watch the tulips grow,
Then I'd end my spell back home in my bed.

Lucy English (13)
The Minster College

THE COUNTRY COLLECTOR

I know a person who collects countries,
I do not know why or how she gets them in
her suitcase,
On the plane,
Or in her house?
But I, myself questioned the country collector,
When and how and why?
She answered,
'Ah you're wrong,
Wrong again,
I don't take countries,
I take some stuff,
No trees nor houses'
So I went home and I thought it out,
'Ha ha' said I,
I know why,
'Cause I saw no country of a sort,
Just,
Foreign food,
Foreign cans,
Weird names on money,
Weird designs of clothing,
Long, funny language books and maps,
Rocked gifts,
Country brochures,
Old information leaflets,
All so well preserved,
But really, why bother,
No point at all,

The food goes mouldy,
So do cans,
And so does money with Sangria spilt,
Not up to me,
Anyway,
Let any country stay at her home,
Any day!

Jaimie Phillips (11)
The Minster College

I KNOW MY TEACHER'S A WITCH

I know my teacher's a witch at least I think I do!
She has long knotted black hair, long razor sharp nails,
And a face as white as the moon.
She has you know, a vicious black cat,
Whose fur is all matted and his ears are scabby and torn.
She worries me! For she wears all black.
Large black pointy shoes, and a long ankle length dress,
To hide her frog-like, wrinkled body.

At school she doesn't say a lot,
As her voice is as sharp as glass.
But when she does speak a cold shiver runs down my spine.
She has those fiery red eyes that seem to glow,
And could put you in a trance.
And when she thinks she's all alone,
She picks the spiders off their webs.
She looks at them for a while,
Then laughs and eats them.

Kim Jones (13)
The Minster College

A PEACEFUL IRELAND

The cease-fire has come,
To our neighbouring country,
The green lands of Ireland.

Each party talks, to another,
To make sure that the peace,
And tranquillity stays with them.

The whole world watches
And hopes that Ireland will
Never hear of a bomb again.

They all hope, that their
Next generation will have,
Loving and peaceful lives.

Lucy Hill (15)
The Minster College

THE TEACHER FROM DOOM

Our teacher is a vampire hating the light.
Waiting for you to forget your homework
to suck your blood.
He is watching your every move.
So be careful, you have been warned.
So please don't forget your homework.
You will be the next lunch.

Lucy Thomas (13)
The Minster College

THE MOON

The moon is a silver coin
Shining brightly in the sky

It is a white bowl
Like a bright cloud in the sky

It is a grey ball
Like a rock in the sky

It is a bright light
Like a round lightbulb in the sky

It is a silver milk top
Like a face in the sky.

Zoe Fletcher (13)
The Minster College

THE MOON

The moon is a bright ball shining
Like a coin in the sky.
It is round and white like a plate.
It reminds me of the silver top
of a milk bottle.
It sometimes reminds me of
a banana because of its shape.
It looks like a blank clock face.

Amanda Dyer (13)
The Minster College